ROBERT WINSTON

THE STORY OF
SCIENCE

ROBERT WINSTON

THE STORY OF
SCIENCE

How science and technology
changed the world

Illustrated by Caitlin Keegan

CONTENTS

INTRODUCTION

Humanity has always sought and found the answers to questions and problems such as how to make our lives easier, how to develop means by which to explore, how to understand and explain the world around us, and more. In many ways, this is the story of science.

Homo sapiens, our species, has been on the planet for around 100,000 years. Our recent ancestors were almost identical to us anatomically and looked very similar, but certainly thought very differently to us. This book is really the story of how that thinking changed.

Much is guesswork, because our early ancestors left no writing, and we can only try to interpret their "records" – scratchings they left on pebbles or bones, or mostly unintelligible marks on cave walls.

For two million years, earlier ancestors made and slowly improved stone hand axes, but never seemed to consider what would seem obvious to you or me – to attach a stick to them to make them more effective. When our ancestors finally did this, it probably happened in different places around the same time.

We see this pattern in the history of new ideas. Many scientific advances

occur at similar times in history, following the needs, culture, threats, or opportunities presented. In this book, you will find many advances from the time humans settled in Mesopotamia, when knowledge started to spread much more rapidly. Many ideas that we presume are more modern were already considered there. Some peoples, of course, were ahead in their development at different periods.

Advances are seldom made by one person, or even one group of people. In this book, I will have certainly attributed some important contributions mistakenly to just one famous individual. Many scientists agree that the most

scientifically valuable room in our place of work is often not the laboratory or the lecture theatre, but the room where we drink coffee together. We are also fortunate to attend frequent gatherings of other scientists. There, social experiences and jokes are shared, and we become aware of the thoughts and problems affecting our colleagues. We often forget those conversations when we get home, yet those ideas are frequently considered later. Then, refreshed, we may address the questions we had previously been considering in our earlier work. This process of collaboration is one of the reasons science is so exciting – it's like a story that never ends.

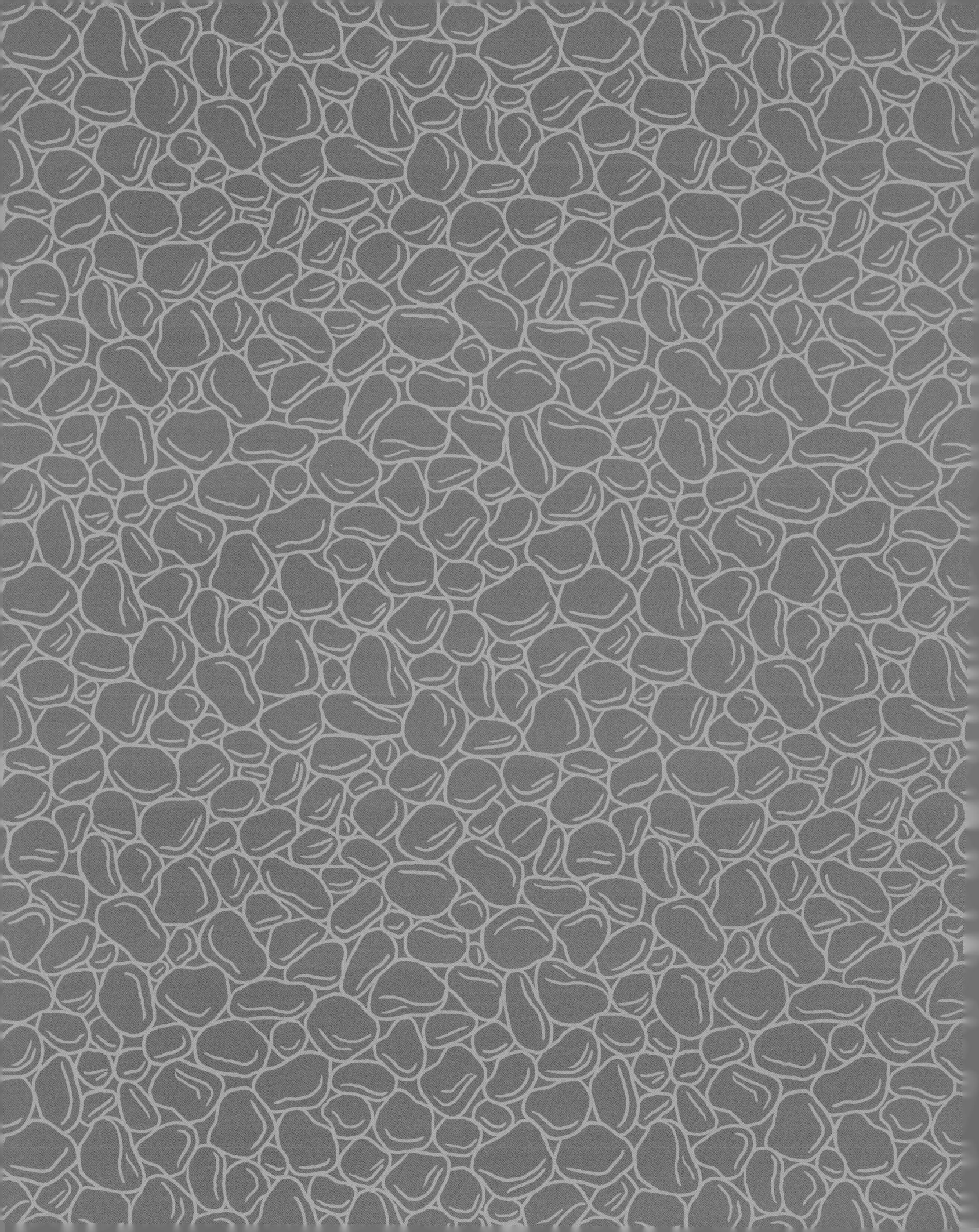

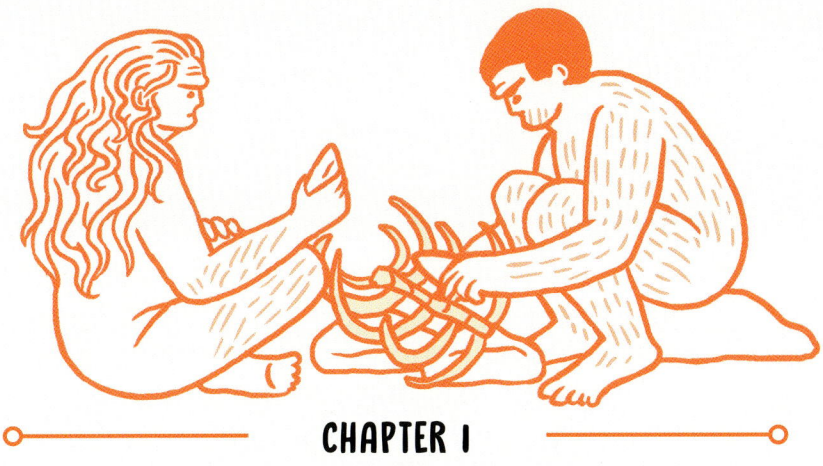

CHAPTER 1

TOOLS

Neither a scientist nor an inventor would be anything without their tools. The first tools that early humans used were much simpler than the ones we use today, but they were very important nonetheless.

The stone hand axe allowed humans to cut meat from bones and to break the bones open to suck out bone marrow. This food changed how our brains developed over time. Humans became more skilled with their hands as they learned to make and use more tools, and we developed fingers and thumbs that could perform more and more complicated tasks. We eventually came to create delicate glass lenses, which made things appear bigger to our eyes. We built the lenses into new tools and were able to witness the wonders of the universe up close and to examine the delicate structures of nature. With modern scientific knowledge, perhaps we may change ourselves even more.

THE STONE HAND AXE

A pointy rock was the single most important invention that humans ever made.

When listing the most important inventions of all time, a lot of people tend to think of things like the wheel, the printing press, or the computer. Though these devices have improved countless lives, the invention that in my opinion tops them all is something simpler – the stone hand axe.

At first glance, the hand axe is just a piece of rock that our ancestors made pointier around 1.8 million years ago. But with this early tool came the ability to hunt. Before, we could only eat things we found growing in nature, such as nuts and berries. Eating meat changed how our brains developed, making them bigger. Through using the hand axe and the tools that followed, and with our newly increased brain power, our hands became better at building and making. So, our progress continued.

Without the stone hand axe, it's unlikely that anything that followed would have been possible.

How was it made?

Hand axes were made by striking flint with a smooth round rock called a hammerstone to create sharp edges. The maker then used a softer hammer, often made of bone or antler to refine the shape. Humans made hand axes in this way for almost two million years.

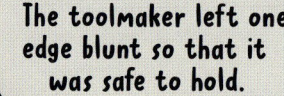

The toolmaker left one edge blunt so that it was safe to hold.

Sharp point

What came next?

Brain development

The hand axe allowed humans to move from being scavengers to skilled hunters. The meat contained vital protein and fats, which would lead to the development of the modern human brain.

Dexterity

Making hand axes helped to build the brain in other ways, by increasing the neurons needed for dexterity – the skill of using your hands. Humans slowly became able to use their opposable finger and thumb for more complex tasks.

More tools

Eventually we could adapt the hand axe into more effective tools, such as axes with handles and throwing spears. These tools helped humans hunt more effectively and safely, and protect themselves from predators.

Hand axes were used to dig, to open nuts, and for hunting.

Hand axes allowed early humans to carve flesh off animal bones so nothing went to waste.

Wheelbarrow

The bar that a wheel turns around, called the axle, is the fulcrum for this lever machine. The load is therefore placed between the effort and the fulcrum, but the lever has the same effect – the load is easier to carry.

The first wheelbarrows were invented in ancient China.

Pyramid lever machine

There are no records showing what the lever machines used to build the pyramids looked like – but a smaller machine of the time that is still used in Egypt today, called a shaduf, gives an idea. The shaduf has a wooden frame serving as the fulcrum, and the arm can swing the load around, as well as lift it.

LEVERS

"Give me a lever, and I can move the world."
Archimedes (c.287–212 BCE)

One of the first machines that humans invented was very simple, but ingenious nonetheless.

Faced with the problem of heavy lifting, people figured out that a long stick could be balanced on some kind of point (which we now call a fulcrum) and wedged underneath the load. The other end of the stick (called the arm) could then be pushed or pulled downwards to lift the load easily off the ground – if the arm was longer, and the force was applied towards the end of it. This contraption was the lever, and it became central to many inventions throughout history.

In ancient Egypt, powerful pharaohs ordered the making of pyramids up to 139 m (456 ft) high. The workers needed the help of machines to lift

The lever balances or turns on a point called a fulcrum.

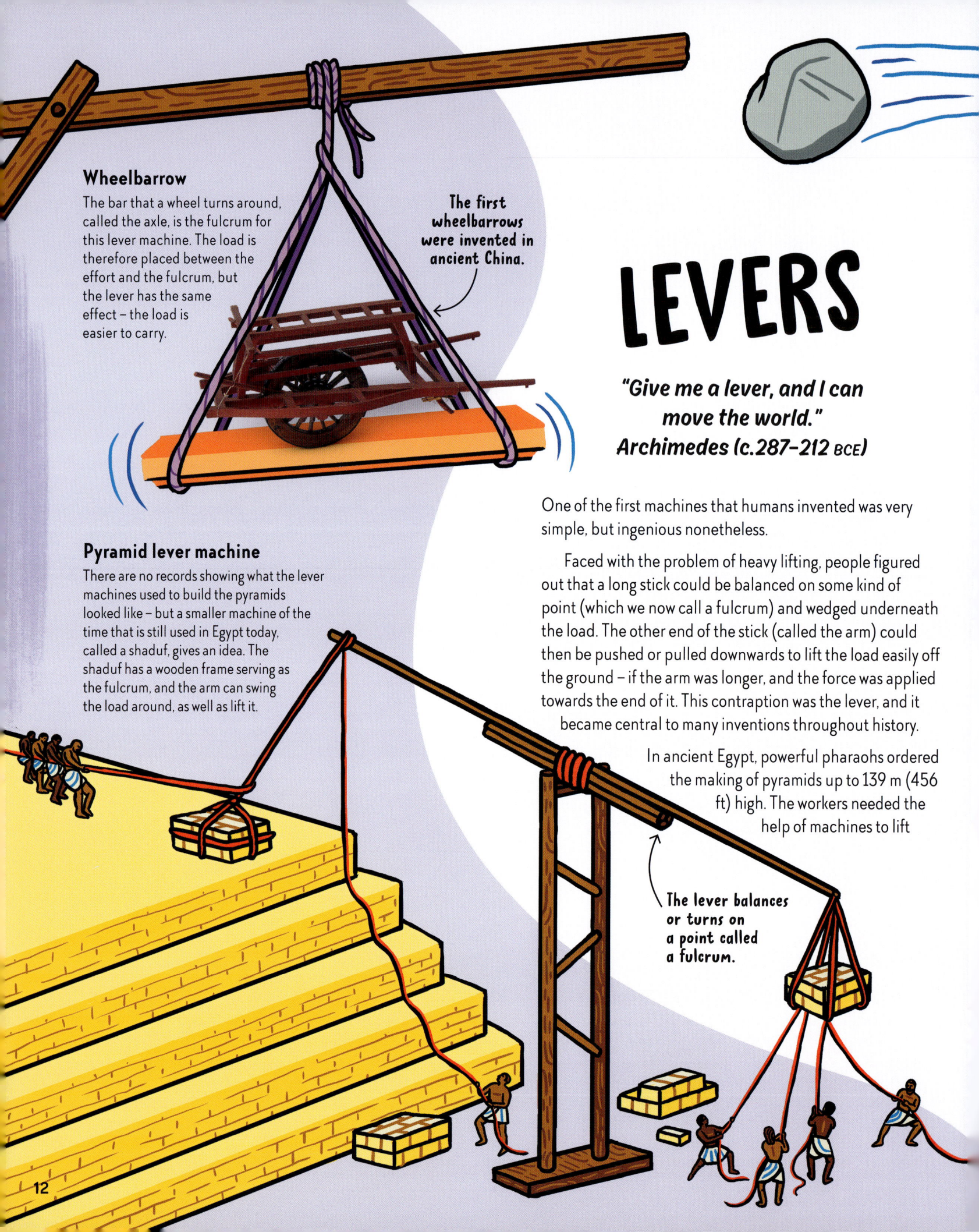

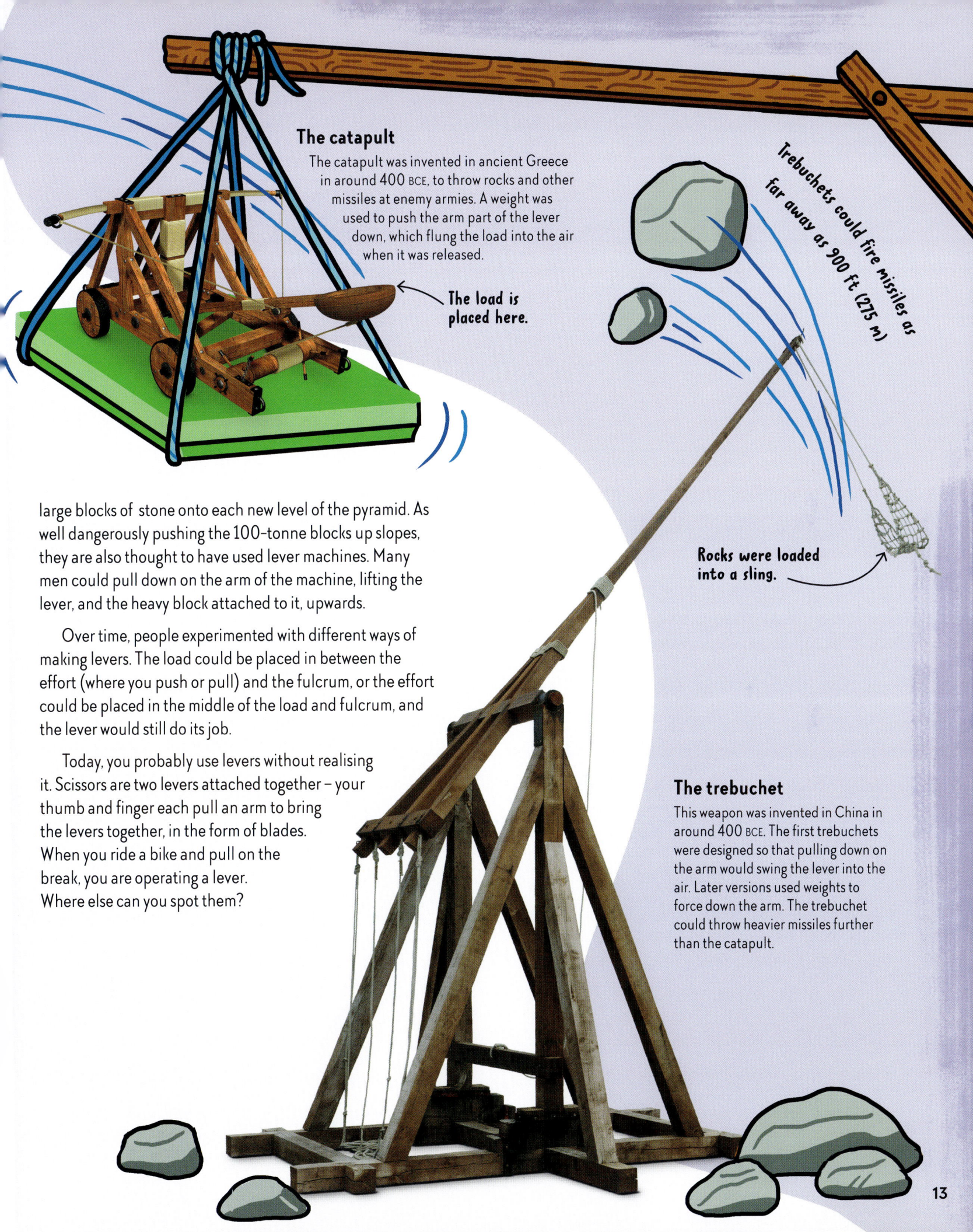

The catapult

The catapult was invented in ancient Greece in around 400 BCE, to throw rocks and other missiles at enemy armies. A weight was used to push the arm part of the lever down, which flung the load into the air when it was released.

The load is placed here.

Trebuchets could fire missiles as far away as 900 ft (275 m)

Rocks were loaded into a sling.

large blocks of stone onto each new level of the pyramid. As well dangerously pushing the 100-tonne blocks up slopes, they are also thought to have used lever machines. Many men could pull down on the arm of the machine, lifting the lever, and the heavy block attached to it, upwards.

Over time, people experimented with different ways of making levers. The load could be placed in between the effort (where you push or pull) and the fulcrum, or the effort could be placed in the middle of the load and fulcrum, and the lever would still do its job.

Today, you probably use levers without realising it. Scissors are two levers attached together – your thumb and finger each pull an arm to bring the levers together, in the form of blades. When you ride a bike and pull on the break, you are operating a lever. Where else can you spot them?

The trebuchet

This weapon was invented in China in around 400 BCE. The first trebuchets were designed so that pulling down on the arm would swing the lever into the air. Later versions used weights to force down the arm. The trebuchet could throw heavier missiles further than the catapult.

TOOLS

A tool is a device or a piece of equipment that is used for a particular purpose. From Stone Age hunting spears, right on through to medical surgery lasers, tools have been developed and utilised by humankind for millions of years.

COOKING AND EATING TOOLS

For much of history, cooking was done over fires or in enclosed clay ovens or pits. In 1444, an Italian duke, the Duke of Urbino, insisted that everybody in his palace use a fork for eating food. Now, cutlery is used in many places around the world.

HUNTING TOOLS

Early humans dug pits to trap animals. Handheld tools only came later, so weighty stones were used to stun or kill. We learned to fish from around 40,000 years ago, probably using spears. Nets were invented to capture large amounts of fish.

FARMING TOOLS

Handheld farming tools, such as blades for cutting crops to be harvested, have been used for thousands of years. And we must not forget how working animals helped to improve farming by pulling along ploughs. Now, motorised tractors pull ploughs and combine harvesters can quickly cut down fields of crops.

MEASURING TOOLS

The first measuring tool was the human body! Hands, feet, and forearms could all be used to measure. Nowadays, scientists use machines to find the size of miniscule strands of DNA, but everyday tools, such as the ones shown here, measure larger lengths, temperature, and weight.

CUTTING TOOLS

Initially, stone tools were crude. By the time the Stone Age ended, meticulous craftsmen were using metal to make delicate knives and razors that could slice with accuracy. Modern cutting tools use diamond – the hardest known mineral – to produce the sharpest blades to date.

The idea to make diamond-coated cutting tools was first thought up in 1862.

CREATIVE TOOLS

Is the greatest creative tool the paint brush? Perhaps it is the musical instrument? Art and science are two great achievements of the human mind, so it's no wonder that scientific thought has furthered the development of creativity.

MEDICAL TOOLS

The first specialised medical tool was the stethoscope, invented by René Laennec in 1819. Embarrassed to place his ear directly onto a lady's chest, he made a paper tube that he put to his ear to hear her heart beating. Needles for injecting vaccines were invented in the same century.

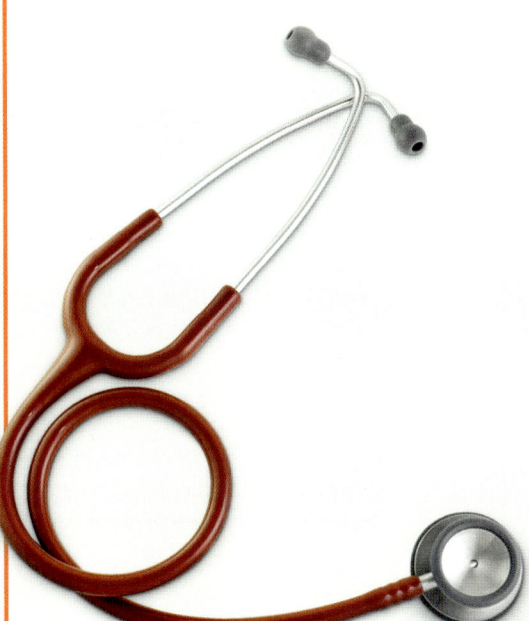

CONSTRUCTION TOOLS

The tools we use for construction mostly function in a similar way to those employed by early builders. Nails are knocked into overlapping pieces of wood to fix them together, or screws are twisted in using a screwdriver. However, the materials we use are changing, to lightweight-yet-strong metals and plastics.

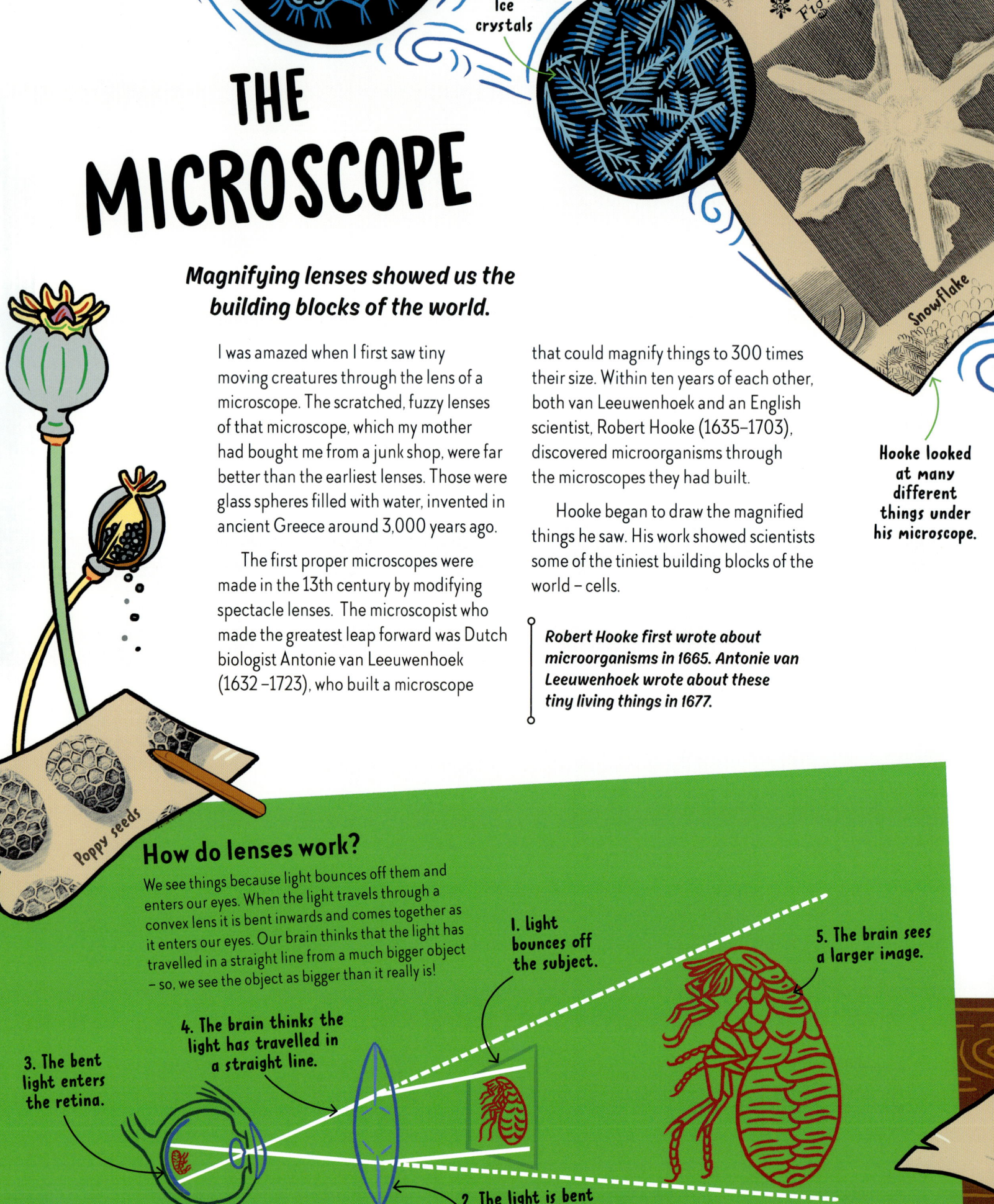

Ice crystals

Fig: 3

Snowflake

THE MICROSCOPE

Magnifying lenses showed us the building blocks of the world.

I was amazed when I first saw tiny moving creatures through the lens of a microscope. The scratched, fuzzy lenses of that microscope, which my mother had bought me from a junk shop, were far better than the earliest lenses. Those were glass spheres filled with water, invented in ancient Greece around 3,000 years ago.

The first proper microscopes were made in the 13th century by modifying spectacle lenses. The microscopist who made the greatest leap forward was Dutch biologist Antonie van Leeuwenhoek (1632–1723), who built a microscope that could magnify things to 300 times their size. Within ten years of each other, both van Leeuwenhoek and an English scientist, Robert Hooke (1635–1703), discovered microorganisms through the microscopes they had built.

Hooke began to draw the magnified things he saw. His work showed scientists some of the tiniest building blocks of the world – cells.

Robert Hooke first wrote about microorganisms in 1665. Antonie van Leeuwenhoek wrote about these tiny living things in 1677.

Hooke looked at many different things under his microscope.

Poppy seeds

How do lenses work?

We see things because light bounces off them and enters our eyes. When the light travels through a convex lens it is bent inwards and comes together as it enters our eyes. Our brain thinks that the light has travelled in a straight line from a much bigger object – so, we see the object as bigger than it really is!

1. light bounces off the subject.

5. The brain sees a larger image.

4. The brain thinks the light has travelled in a straight line.

3. The bent light enters the retina.

2. The light is bent through the lens.

Flea

Stone

MICROGRAPHIA

In 1665, Robert Hooke published a book of his microscopic drawings, called *Micrographia*. One page described how plants were made up of tiny, walled segments – which he called "cells", after the cells in honeycomb.

Charcoal

Barrel

light from this oil lamp was focused onto the specimen under the microscope to help Hooke see every detail.

A sphere containing water spread the light out across the specimen.

What came next?

Cell biology

Knowing that our bodies are made up of different types of cell has allowed scientists to figure out how certain illnesses work, and to find ways to heal them. Using modern technology, scientists have been able to change the behaviour of cells in the human body that might otherwise cause cancer.

lens

HOOKE'S MICROSCOPE

Specimen

Arthropods

Cork

I INVENTED IT!

Hans lipperhey

THE TELESCOPE

This invention showed us the wonders of space.

In 1608, Dutch spectacle maker Hans Lipperhey designed a device that would make far-away objects appear bigger to the eye. But it was Italian astronomer Galileo Galilei who made history with this invention, called the telescope.

Galileo heard about Hans' design and built his own version in 1609, which he turned to the stars. He observed four objects moving in a curved line around Jupiter. He took these to be stars, but we now know that they are moons. Galileo's finding was the great proof that our Earth is not at the centre of the universe, with everything orbiting around it, as most people believed at the time.

Galileo asked the Doge of Venice for money to refine his instrument. He pointed out that it could be used to help defend Venice, as enemy ships off the coast could be spotted two hours sooner than with the naked eye. The money was granted, and Galileo's second telescope showed celestial bodies in even greater detail, such as the craters on the surface of the moon.

Galileo sketched what he saw through his telescope, and these drawings helped people begin to understand space.

I MADE IT BETTER!

Galileo

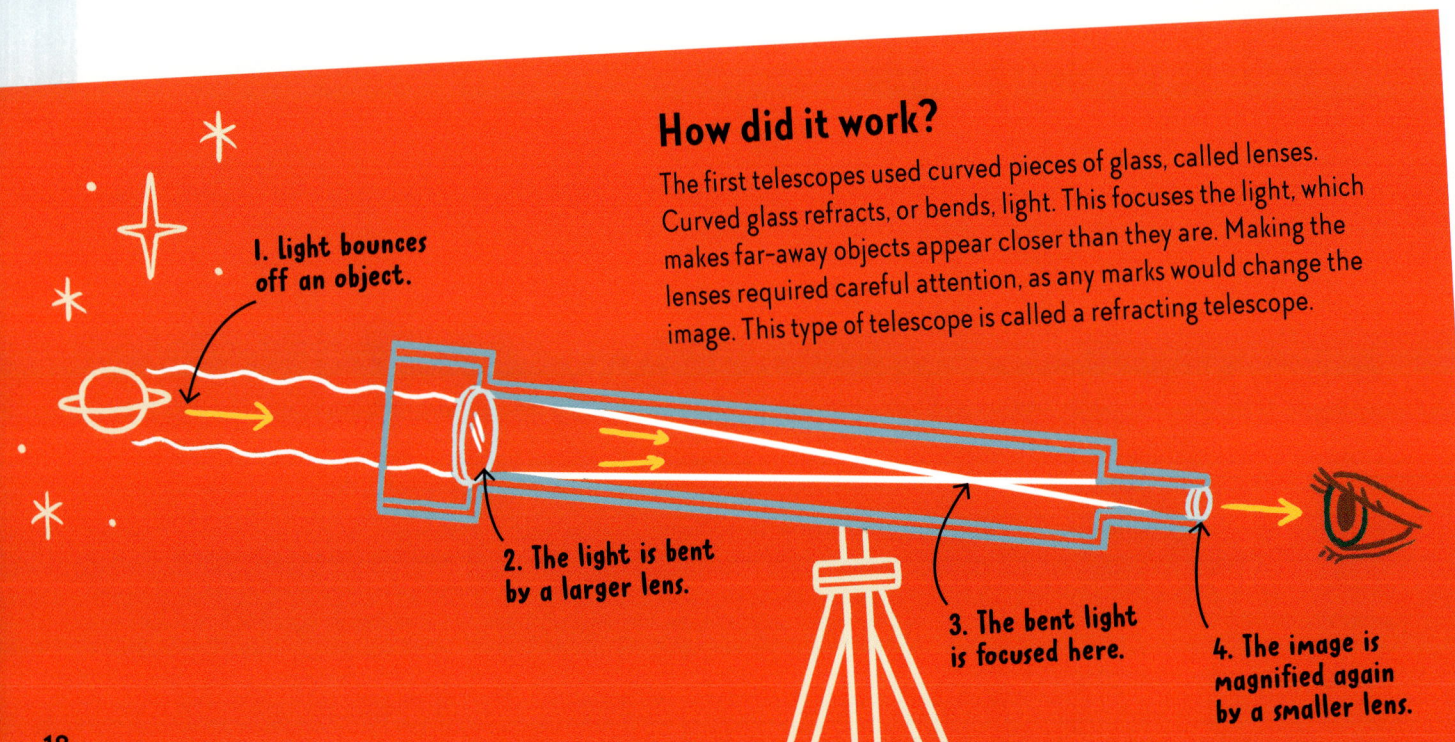

How did it work?

The first telescopes used curved pieces of glass, called lenses. Curved glass refracts, or bends, light. This focuses the light, which makes far-away objects appear closer than they are. Making the lenses required careful attention, as any marks would change the image. This type of telescope is called a refracting telescope.

1. light bounces off an object.

2. The light is bent by a larger lens.

3. The bent light is focused here.

4. The image is magnified again by a smaller lens.

What came next?

Reflecting telescopes

The English astronomer Isaac Newton developed the first reflecting telescope in 1668. Newton realised that light is focused when it bounces off a mirror. So, instead of lenses, he built a telescope using mirrors – which could more easily be made smooth than lenses. Mirrors flip images back to front, so the telescope had other mirrors inside it to flip the image the right way around again.

Newton's telescope

1. light bounces off an object.

2. A large mirror reflects light from the lens.

3. A small mirror flips the image from the large mirror into the eyepiece.

Galileo's earlier telescopes made distant objects appear three times bigger. His later telescopes showed objects 30 times bigger!

Radio images

In 1937, US astronomer Grote Reber designed the first telescope that picked up radio waves, rather than light. Planets, comets, and other objects in space emit these waves. Radio waves can be studied to work out what a celestial body is made of and how it moves. Unlike light, clouds do not block out radio waves.

Radio telescope

Sliding tube to improve the focus

Eyepiece

TWO OF GALILEO'S TELESCOPES

TVBVM OPTICVM VIDES GALILÆII INVENTVM, ET OPVS, QVO SOLIS MACVLAS, ET EXTIMOS LVNÆ MONTES, ET IOVIS SATELLITES, ET NOVAM QVASI RERVM VNIVERSITATE PRIMVS DISPEXIT A. MDCIX.

Telescopes in space

The Hubble Space Telescope began orbiting the Earth in 1990, at a distance of 332 miles (535 km) from the ground. The telescope's camera could take pictures that were 10 times clearer than any telescope on Earth. Stars and other galaxies could now be studied in greater detail than ever before.

CHAPTER 2

ART AND CULTURE

Artistic achievements, new inventions, and scientific discoveries are all part of our species' natural genius. But we sometimes forget that these topics are linked.

Creative minds are needed to come up with scientific ideas. These ideas could not be written down, shared, and proven right or wrong if we had not created writing systems. Without television, ideas could not be further spread, and young scientists might not be inspired to explore the science of the future.

Inventions have allowed us to be more creative. Tens of thousands of years ago, people improved their musical skills with bones hollowed out to make early flutes. Science, too, is at the heart of many types of cultural activities and art. Scientific experiments can lead to new, striking colours of paint. And the science of DNA helps us to understand the cultures of the past.

HANDPRINTS ON WALLS

There are more than 200 handprints in total on the walls of the Caves of Gargas in modern-day France. The paint to make the handprints was made from water mixed with pigments such as brown ochre and black charcoal. A hollow reed may have been used to spray paint evenly over the hands.

CAVES OF GARGAS, FRANCE

Some of the handprints had long and short fingers.

RELIGION

Long before science, religion was our way of trying to understand the world.

20,000 years ago, a group of humans in what is now France filled their mouths with paint, placed their hands on the walls of a cave, and blew. Many of the handprints they made looked as though fingers had been cut off. Archaeologists now think that these fingers were bent down to create different shapes. But why? Perhaps these symbols were part of an early religion.

A clue to what the handprints meant can be found in the signals made by some modern hunter gatherers. On the hunt, people might signal silently to others joining them – two fingers raised could mean they are tracking a horned animal, one a rabbit, and none could mean that an elephant is close by.

JUDAISM

This religion began around 4,000 years ago, in what is now Israel. Followers of Judaism believe that a single God created the world. A symbol of Judaism is the menorah – a candelabra with seven candles.

HINDUISM

The first Hindus lived in India more than 2,500 years ago. Hindus believe in many different gods. The Hindu symbol shown here means "aum" – a sound which represents creation and other ideas.

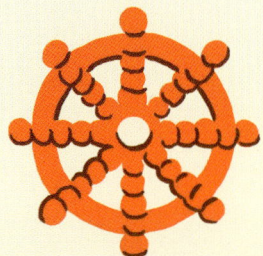

BUDDHISM

This religion is based on the teachings of the Buddha, who is thought to have been born in Nepal in around 500 BCE. The Wheel of Dharma is a key Buddhist symbol. It represents the Buddha's teachings.

RELIGIOUS BUILDINGS

Caves may have been some of the first religious places of worship. Over time, many amazing structures were built so that people could honour their gods. The largest religious structure in the world is the Buddhist temple complex, Angkor Wat, which covers 400 acres (160 hectares).

Science and religion are both ways to try to explain and understand the world, and at times this has caused them to come into conflict with each other.

Like modern hand signals, the handprints may represent animals. Sprayed on the cave wall, the animals could have been left for some spirit or power that people believed controlled the world – to ask for a good hunt. Stone Age people may have believed that rituals like this helped them to survive. They relied on wild food, and they would starve if they couldn't find animals or edible plants to sustain them. And they would frequently have been bitterly cold and without clothes. Life was tough, so perhaps religion helped them to hope for better times. Just one successful hunt of a large animal could provide weeks of food and skins for warmth.

When Stone Age people thought about the world, and began to come up with explanations and ideas to help themselves, they were behaving like scientists. Both science and religion are ways of understanding the world for modern people. The religions with the largest followings today are shown below.

ANGKOR WAT, CAMBODIA

Religious buildings are often made from expensive stone and painted with beautiful designs.

CHRISTIANITY

Christians follow the teachings of Jesus, who lived around 2,000 years ago. Jesus died nailed to a wooden cross, which is why the cross is a symbol. Christians believe in one God, the father of Jesus.

ISLAM

Muslims believe in one God and follow the teachings of the prophet Muhammad, who was born in the 500s. A crescent moon and star are sometimes used as symbols of Islam on flags and buildings.

SIKHISM

This religion began around 500 years ago in South Asia. Sikhs follow the teachings of Guru Nanak and the nine gurus that came after him. Their symbol, the Khanda, represents knowledge.

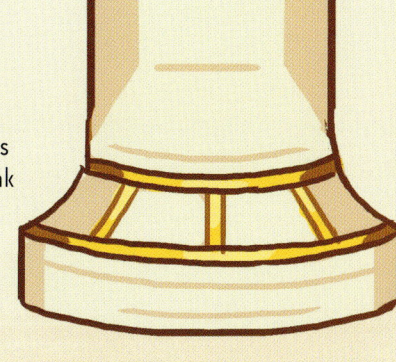

THE FLUTE

People made use of the science of music and enjoyed its sounds as far back as 35,000 years ago.

Music is a creative art, but it is a science too. Musical instruments work because of the size, shape, and spacing of their various parts, which determine the sounds they produce. The oldest surviving musical instruments are flutes, and some of them date from the Stone Age, which began before modern humans existed.

The oldest flutes, from around 35,000 years ago, were found in caves in China and Europe, and are made of bone, pierced with holes. Scientists believe that the reason flutes are the oldest surviving instruments is that other instruments were made of perishable materials, such as string or reeds, so they degraded over time.

Bone flutes tell us a lot about the people who made them: they used stone tools, they understood at least some of the science of sound, and – perhaps most important of all – they valued music.

Music and other creative pursuits are often signs of a civilised society. Once primitive survival needs are met, a flourishing society has time to appreciate the arts. Discovering that music was enjoyed in the Stone Age shows us that even back then, there was more to life than just hunting and gathering.

What came next?

THE DIVJE BABE FLUTE

In 1995, archaeologists at the Divje Babe cave in Slovenia discovered a bone pierced with holes. It was a Stone Age flute created by Neanderthals – making it the oldest musical instrument ever found!

The Divje Babe flute was made from the femur (thigh bone) of a cave bear cub.

How does it work?

When air is blown across the flute's mouthpiece it vibrates, producing sound waves. The vibrations depend on the proportions of the flute. The pitch of the note is determined by the tube's length and the strength of the musician's blowing. Closing the holes of the flute changes the note that is played.

Sound waves

Sound waves are channelled into our ears, which convert them into nerve signals that we hear as music.

Recorded music

Thomas Edison invented the phonograph in 1887 to record and replay sounds. It gathered sound waves in its cone but the quality of the recording wasn't great. In the 1920s, electrical microphones made recorded music much, much better.

Written music

The earliest examples of written music were found on a Mesopotamian tablet from 1400 BCE. Writing down the sounds of music shows that music held an important place in Mesopotamian culture.

Electronic music

Nowadays, music itself can be created electronically, so some might argue there's no need for musical instruments that are lovingly crafted to produce pitch-perfect sound waves. Musicians might disagree though!

It made people see Neanderthals in a whole new light!

This find was the first indication that Neanderthals created music.

PIGMENTS

The science of colour-making changed art forever.

Red ochre

This mineral can be found in soil. Around 65,000 years ago, people began crushing it into powder to make paint. Some early ochre works of art show animals and handprints.

The ochre paintings in Lascaux Cave, France, were made c.20,000 years ago.

Vermillion

This reddish pigment, from the mineral cinnabar, has been used around the world since around 8000 BCE. Statues from ancient Greece are white now but were once painted with pigments including vermillion, which faded with time.

Cinnabar

Tens of thousands of years ago, early people figured out that the colours they saw in precious stones and bright red berries could be extracted and used to make art. Over time, people learned to find colours in all kinds of places and, eventually, to make them using chemicals.

Pigments, including black from burned wood and yellow from the mineral ochre, were used from around 30,000 years ago to draw pictures on the walls of caves. Pigments are not easily dissolved in water, so these images were not washed away by rain or running water.

People later learned to make dyes, which dissolve in water and can be used to colour cloth. A very old piece of indigo cloth showed that this colour was being used by about 4000 BCE in Peru. The dye was extracted from certain leaves. Another ancient dye was taken from the slime of a species of snail – this purple dye was used to colour the cloaks of Roman leaders. Other dyes were taken from berries. Mulberries are tasty, but be careful – their juice can stain clothes dark red.

Why do we see colours?

Sunlight is made up of different colours of light, each with a different wavelength. Dyes and pigments work by absorbing certain wavelengths of visible light. The rest of the light is scattered away, giving the colour we see.

Prussian blue

This pigment was the result of an experiment gone wrong. A chemist trying to make red pigment noticed that animal oil had gotten into a batch, and it was changing the colour to a deep blue.

During the Renaissance (1300s–1600s), a deep blue taken from the lapis lazuli stone and used to make paint became the world's most expensive pigment.

The artists that use colour are excellent scientists. They experiment, fail, and succeed in making new colours, by mixing existing shades. Blue plus yellow gives various green colours depending on the amount of each material they use.

Today, many pigments and dyes are made by mixing chemicals in laboratories. They can be worth a lot of money. More than $400 million each year is spent on the red paint used on Ferrari cars. A pure white pigment taken from the metal titanium is worth much more.

The Statue of Liberty

Green copper

Copper starts off browny red but turns green-blue if it is exposed to the air for a long time. This is how the Statue of Liberty in New York, USA, got its colour. The greenish pigment that comes from air-exposed copper is called verdigris. During the Middle Ages (c.500–1500), painters made the pigment by exposing copper to vinegar, causing a greenish layer to form on the copper's surface.

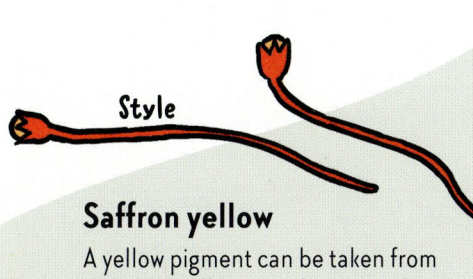

Style

Saffron yellow

A yellow pigment can be taken from the spice saffron. It is found on the tips of a saffron crocus flower's styles. This pigment has been used for around 50,000 years. The ancient Greeks and Romans used it to dye their clothes.

Saffron crocus

Pictographs

Pictographic symbols represent an object or a concept such as something which is a notice, general announcement, or communication. They may also refer to a king or ruler, a title, an animal, or an important name. Pictographs can also be religious or refer to historical events.

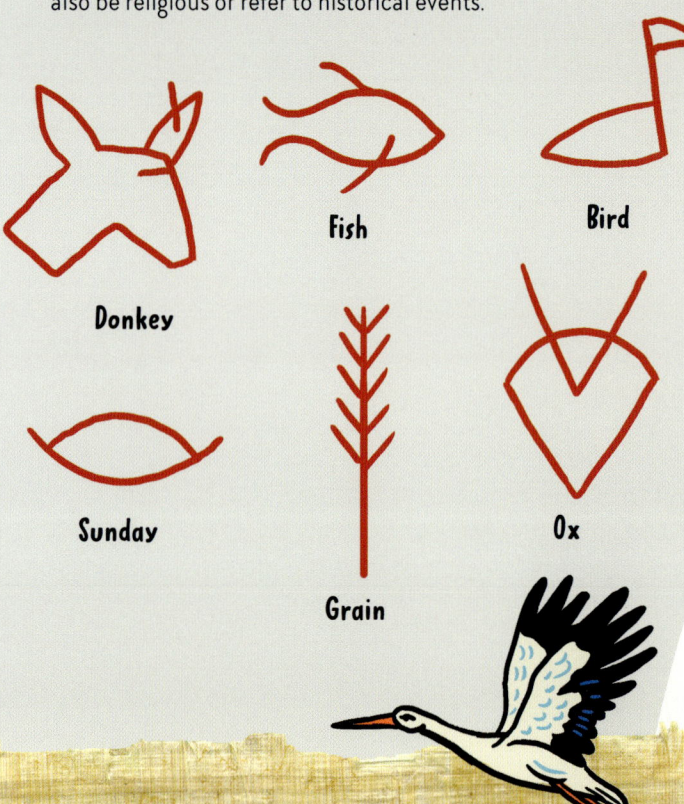

Donkey

Fish

Bird

Sunday

Grain

Ox

Ideographs

Ideographic symbols are abstract symbols that directly represent an idea or concept, but not necessarily the sound from the language. These scripts are also very ancient, and pre-date writing actual words.

To carry

To call

To be old

To fly

WRITING

This way of expressing and recording ideas was by far the most important invention needed for science.

Writing began as a way to agree financial contracts, tell stories, and make poetry. Many experts used to believe all writing began in Mesopotamia, but examples from other areas have now been analysed, and were developed independently at a similar time. Writing began in Egypt around 3250 BCE, in Mesopotamia around 3100 BCE, and in China around 1200 BCE. Other ancient scripts have been found from Easter Island and central Europe, but they have not yet been translated.

Different scripts use different symbols – most ancient ones with pictographs, some with cuneiform symbols, and some different alphabets. Alphabetic writing in a language was invented within a period of around two to three thousand years. This seems long, but historically this was relatively a short period. Homo sapiens had been on the planet for around 100,000 years, and this suggests that humankind innovated at roughly the same stages of existence.

CUNEIFORM TABLET

This cuneiform tablet is from around 2800 BCE, and is a list of supplies of bread and drink. Cuneiform is one of the earliest writing systems.

Pictographs are associated with the earliest writing, and within 1,000 years or so, letters of alphabets followed. These were formed to make sounds (called phonemes) associated with a language.

Some early written languages are undoubtedly related. A good example are the Semitic languages – Phoenician, Canaanite, Amharic, Syriac, Aramaic, Hebrew, and Arabic. These languages are written from right to left using around 20-30 consonants. Vowels were not written, the reader has to know the root word and guess how to pronounce it.

In the history of how writing has evolved, our complex writing systems were preceded by proto-writing and systems of ideographs.

Without writing, scientists could not record what was used for an experiment, its outcome, what went wrong, what was measured mathematically, or how to improve the concept. Good, accurate writing is essential for all proper science.

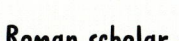

Roman scholar

Logographs

Logographs are sounds or spoken symbols; the form of the symbol or letter is not related to its meaning. A verbal logograph may represent a whole word or just a syllable. Alphabetic logographs may be a single sound made by a letter.

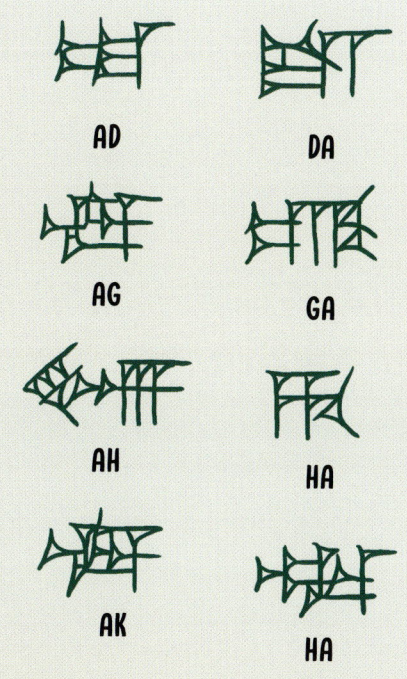

AB

BA

EB

ED

EG

EH

EK

AD

DA

AG

GA

AH

HA

AK

HA

Letters

Around 1500 BCE, people in Canaan, east of Egypt, adapted Egyptian hieroglyphs into a simpler system and created the first alphabet. It was later adapted and expanded by the ancient Greeks and Romans.

TELEVISION

This invention changed the face of entertainment and the way we communicate information.

After the creation of moving pictures in the late 19th century, many inventors tried to work out a way to transmit them into homes. The first person to achieve this was the Scottish inventor John Logie Baird, who created the first "Televisor" in 1926. Baird's machine was quickly replaced by superior technology, but his invention stoked the public's enthusiasm and heralded a new age of entertainment for the next century.

Early television was broadcast in black and white, and while the first colour broadcasts were made in the USA in the 1950s, it wasn't until the 1970s that colour television really took off. Since then, the quality of image and sound has steadily increased.

As well as for entertainment, television is crucial for communication and education. For one thing, some programmes can help people gain a better understanding of science!

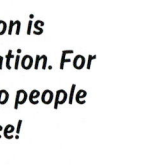

HOME FURNITURE
Baird's television, along with the majority of early television sets, was designed to resemble home furniture, and to be built into metal or wood cabinets.

What came next?

The cathode-ray tube
In 1932, the Radio Corporation of America (RCA) created an all-electric television with a cathode-ray tube in the receiver. It produced a better picture than Baird's mechanical system, and became the standard for televisions for many years to come.

Public television
In 1936, the British Broadcasting Corporation (BBC) began regular public broadcasts in London. Then, in 1939, the Radio Corporation of America (RCA) started America's first fully electronic TV service. By the 1950s, television was replacing radio as the main source of home entertainment.

How did it work?

Baird called his machine a "televisor". It used rotating discs to scan moving images and output them as electric impulses. These impulses were transmitted by cable to the screen, His first broadcast featured a dummy's head that he called Stooky Bill.

Spinning disc

Stooky Bill

Mechanical spinning discs

Small screen

JOHN LOGIE BAIRD'S

WORLD FAMOUS

TELEVISOR

VCR

Sony introduced the first low-cost Video Cassette Recorder (VCR) in 1969, but they became very popular in the 1980s. A VCR could be used to record programmes, so they could be played back again and again. VCRs were eventually replaced by DVD players.

Modern televisions

Over the years, televisions have become bigger and flatter, and the image on-screen is displayed using liquid crystals, rather than the cathode-ray tube. Modern TVs can also connect to the internet and stream shows and films from various online services.

CHAPTER 3

HOW THE WORLD WORKS

You might think that science helps us to understanding everything. But as a scientist doing laboratory experiments, I found that the more things I learnt the less I truly knew.

Each of the subjects in this section tell us something about how the world works, but they also raise wonderful, intriguing questions. In the field of astronomy, powerful telescopes show us stars that are 13 billion light years away, but we don't know what is happening around them in that part of space. Gravity is another puzzle. How does a large mass exert force? And does radiation, such as light, take the form of particles called photons, or waves? The bewildering answer is: "both". The theory of evolution leaves many unanswered questions, too. We have evidence that all species evolved through many generations, but the evolution of the cell – the structure that makes up every species – remains a mystery.

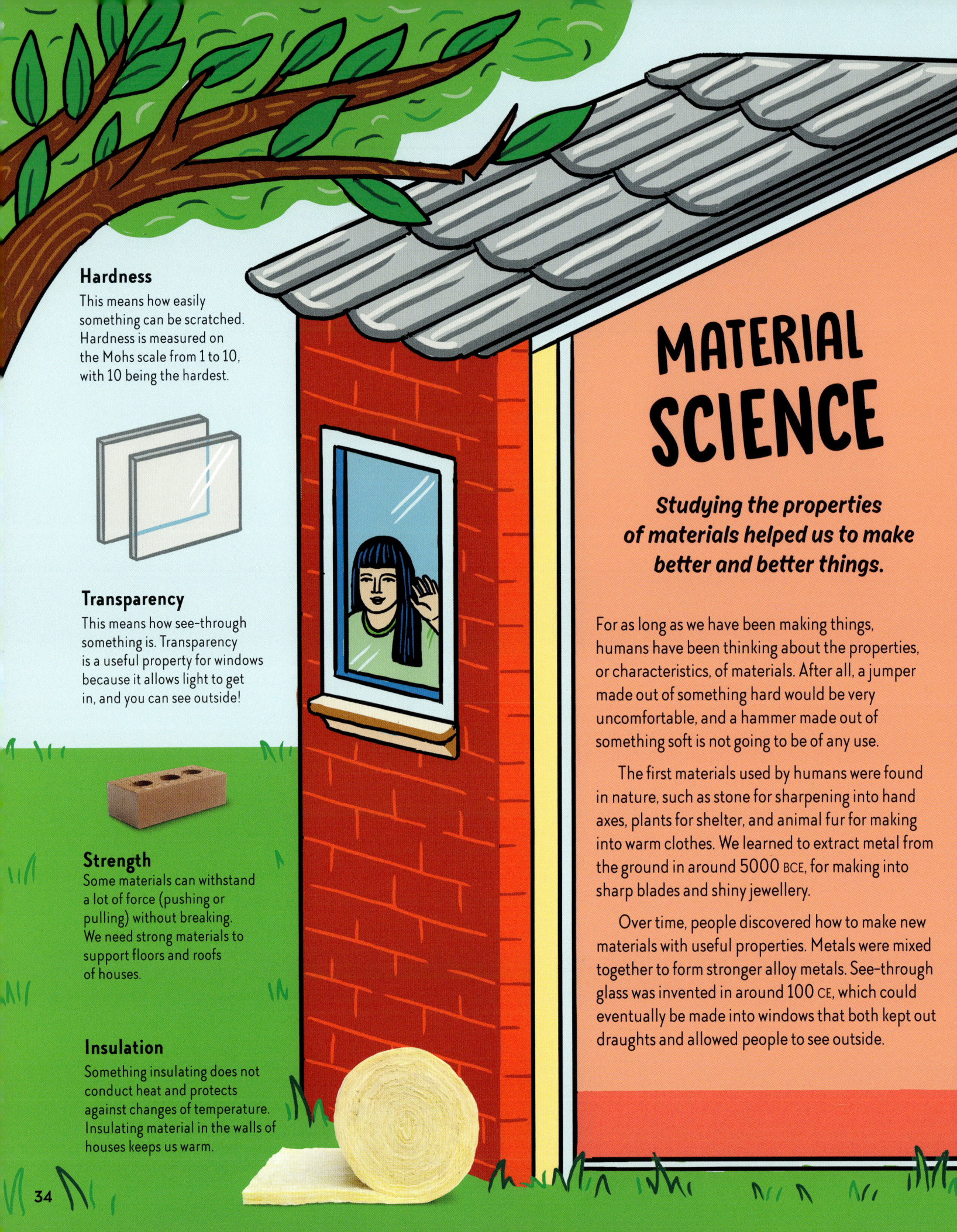

Hardness

This means how easily something can be scratched. Hardness is measured on the Mohs scale from 1 to 10, with 10 being the hardest.

Transparency

This means how see-through something is. Transparency is a useful property for windows because it allows light to get in, and you can see outside!

Strength

Some materials can withstand a lot of force (pushing or pulling) without breaking. We need strong materials to support floors and roofs of houses.

Insulation

Something insulating does not conduct heat and protects against changes of temperature. Insulating material in the walls of houses keeps us warm.

MATERIAL SCIENCE

Studying the properties of materials helped us to make better and better things.

For as long as we have been making things, humans have been thinking about the properties, or characteristics, of materials. After all, a jumper made out of something hard would be very uncomfortable, and a hammer made out of something soft is not going to be of any use.

The first materials used by humans were found in nature, such as stone for sharpening into hand axes, plants for shelter, and animal fur for making into warm clothes. We learned to extract metal from the ground in around 5000 BCE, for making into sharp blades and shiny jewellery.

Over time, people discovered how to make new materials with useful properties. Metals were mixed together to form stronger alloy metals. See-through glass was invented in around 100 CE, which could eventually be made into windows that both kept out draughts and allowed people to see outside.

Mass

The mass of a material means how much matter it contains. Gravity pulls on mass to give an object weight, so objects with more mass weigh more.

Density

This means how much mass an object has for its size. A gold bracelet is denser than a feather of the same size because it has more mass.

A volcanic rock called obsidian was first made into super sharp blades during the Stone Age, and was still used to make scalpels for eye surgery up until the 1980s.

In the 1800s, we worked out that everything is made up of atoms. Materials have now been invented with atoms arranged in special ways to create unique properties – one example is graphene, a form of carbon, which is extremely strong but lightweight.

Material science is an exciting field today. Scientists have made materials that can remember their original shape after being deformed and packaging that can break down in nature, which may help to solve the problem of plastic waste.

Nanoparticles

Very tiny particles less than 100 nanometres in size can give a material new properties. They are so small they cannot be seen with a light microscope. In sunscreen, they can absorb and scatter UV light, preventing sunburn.

Plasticity

If something has plasticity, it can be easily shaped or moulded. Modelling clay has a high level of plasticity.

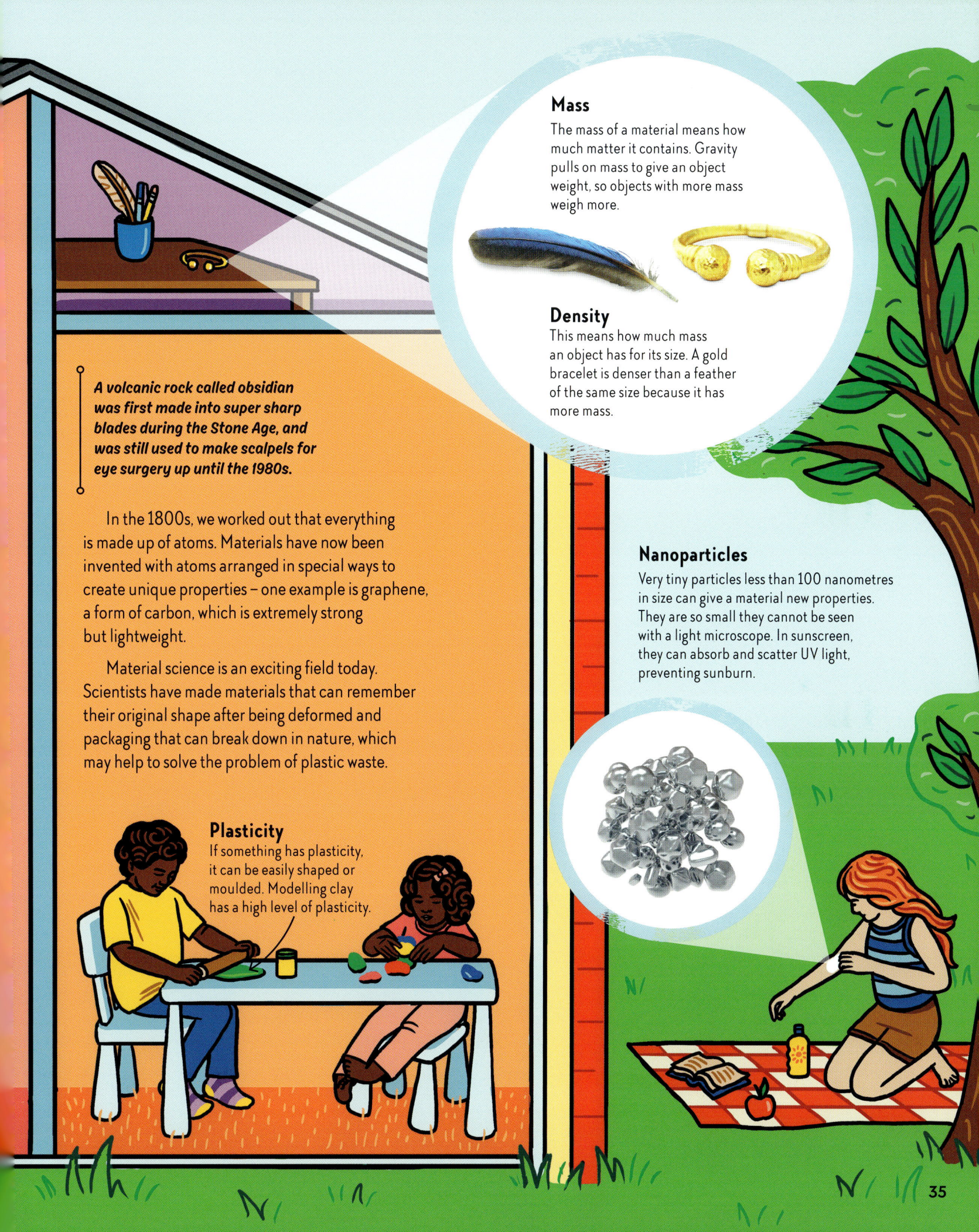

An expanding universe

In 1939, US astronomer Edward Hubble noticed that the most distant galaxies from Earth seemed to be moving further away at a constant rate, in all directions. So, the universe must be expanding outwards. Hubble's evidence supported an earlier idea, from 1920, that our universe exploded outwards from a single ball of matter, in a "Big Bang".

1. The Big Bang

The universe began as "the singularity" – a very hot, very dense ball of matter, which exploded.

2. Atoms

380,000 years after the Big Bang, particles flung out by the explosion began to form into atoms.

3. Stars and galaxies

The first stars formed 180 million years after the Big Bang. Gravity pulled these stars into galaxies within the first billion years.

4. Our solar system

We are relative newcomers to the world – our solar system formed around 8.7 billion years after the Big Bang.

5. Today's universe

You are living 13.8 billion years after the universe began. Our universe continues to expand, and, we learned in 1998, the speed with which it expands is increasing.

MODERN ASTRONOMY

Much of what we know about the universe was learned in the last 100 years.

Is the universe expanding? How do stars form and die? How old are the stars we can see with our bare eyes? These are just some of the questions that ingenious modern physicists have tried to answer, armed with ever more powerful telescopes and some very complicated maths equations.

Perhaps one of the most mysterious discoveries in modern astronomy is that of dark matter. This type of matter is invisible and completely undetectable with any instrument invented so far. But, as with many other things in space, maths allowed us to predict its existence.

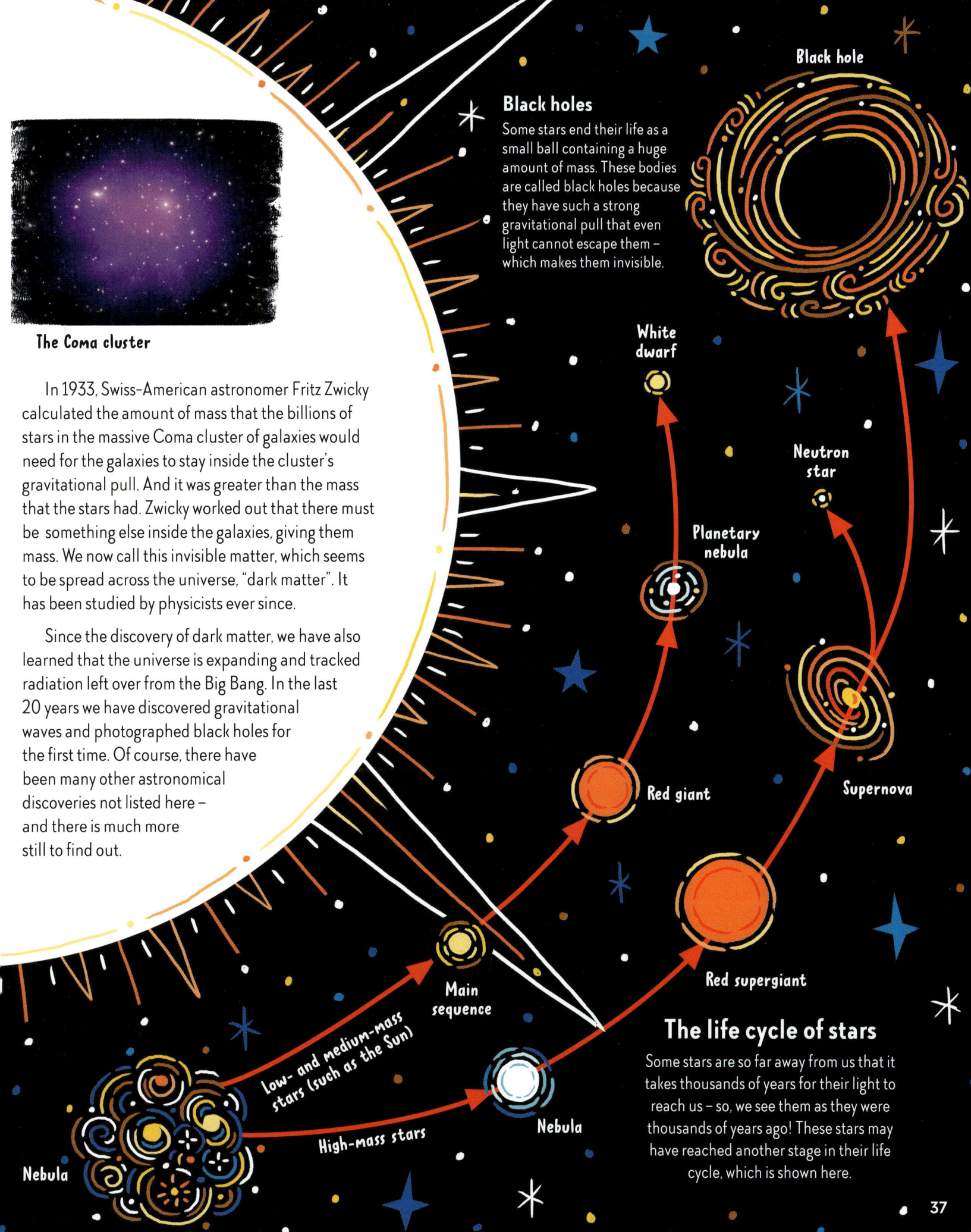

The Coma cluster

In 1933, Swiss-American astronomer Fritz Zwicky calculated the amount of mass that the billions of stars in the massive Coma cluster of galaxies would need for the galaxies to stay inside the cluster's gravitational pull. And it was greater than the mass that the stars had. Zwicky worked out that there must be something else inside the galaxies, giving them mass. We now call this invisible matter, which seems to be spread across the universe, "dark matter". It has been studied by physicists ever since.

Since the discovery of dark matter, we have also learned that the universe is expanding and tracked radiation left over from the Big Bang. In the last 20 years we have discovered gravitational waves and photographed black holes for the first time. Of course, there have been many other astronomical discoveries not listed here – and there is much more still to find out.

Black holes

Some stars end their life as a small ball containing a huge amount of mass. These bodies are called black holes because they have such a strong gravitational pull that even light cannot escape them – which makes them invisible.

Black hole

White dwarf

Neutron star

Planetary nebula

Supernova

Red giant

Red supergiant

Main sequence

Low- and medium-mass stars (such as the Sun)

High-mass stars

Nebula

Nebula

The life cycle of stars

Some stars are so far away from us that it takes thousands of years for their light to reach us – so, we see them as they were thousands of years ago! These stars may have reached another stage in their life cycle, which is shown here.

Isaac Newton

A pandemic plays a part in the story of how Newton came up with his theory of gravity. He had been sent home from university because of the Great Plague when (he claimed) a falling apple in his mother's garden caused him to think about the force that pulled it down. Newton went on to make many more scientific discoveries – including that sunlight is made up of different colours.

Everything has a gravitational pull, but things with more mass have a stronger pull. So, the Earth pulls apples towards it - and not the other way around.

GRAVITY

This mysterious force holds the universe together.

The ancient Greeks believed that everything in the world – earth, fire, water, and air – had a natural position, and that if moved it would fall back into place. It took around another 2,000 years for scientists to get a little closer to the truth about why things fall to Earth.

In the late 1600s, English scientist and mathematician Isaac Newton argued that there was a force pulling objects, such as apples, towards the ground. He later worked out that the same force kept the Moon orbiting around the Earth. He called this force gravity.

Newton often retold the story of how he came up with his theory.

Gravity in space

The Sun pulls our planet, and the other planets in the solar system, towards it. As we are moving through space, this causes our planet to orbit the Sun. In the same way, the Earth's gravity keeps the Moon in orbit.

Gravity helped astronomers to predict the existence of the planet Neptune – they spotted that the orbits of outer planets in our solar system were being affected by the gravity of a planet they could not see.

In 1915, the scientist Albert Einstein changed how we thought about gravity. He worked out that gravity affects light waves and photons, the particles around atoms which make light. In fact, he said that gravity affects all matter and energy moving in spacetime – which is time and space joined together. The gravity from massive objects even distorts spacetime. He also explained that gravity, like light, must come in waves.

The discovery of gravity was a stepping stone to a greater understanding of the universe. Einstein's theory was used to predict the existence of black holes (see page 36), which produce such strong gravitational waves that light can't escape from them. What else might this powerful force tell us about the world?

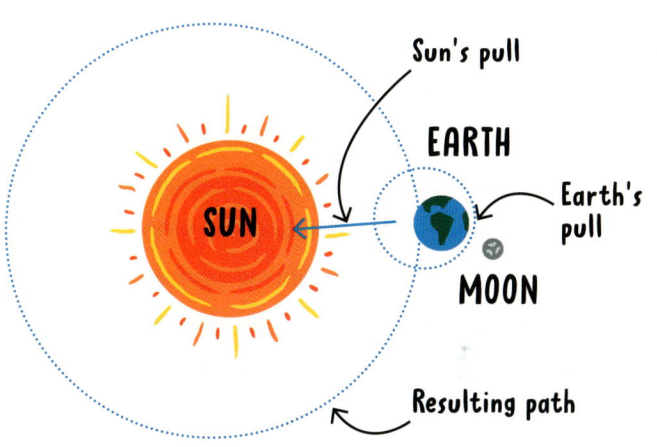

Sun's pull

EARTH

Earth's pull

SUN

MOON

Resulting path

Mechanical models of the solar system, called orreries, became popular in the 1700s.

Without gravity, everything would float away from the Earth - clouds, apples, and you!

Understanding the solar system

In the 1500s, German astronomer Nicolaus Copernicus stated that Earth was not the centre of the universe, as most people believed at the time – he said that a force kept planets stuck in orbit around our Sun. Newton's discovery of gravity was further evidence for Copernicus's idea, and more people began to accept the truth.

The wrong idea

In the 1600s and 1700s, it was thought that things that burnt contained phlogiston. The more phlogiston they contained, the better they burnt. Combustion was then thought to release phlogiston into the air.

PHLOGISTON IN AIR

WOOD
(contains phlogiston)

→ +

ASHES
(no phlogiston)

The German scientist Johann Becher (1635-1682) came up with the phlogiston theory.

COMBUSTION

Learning the ingredients of fire allowed us to use it like never before.

Humans may have known how to make fire millions of years ago, but it wasn't until fairly recently that we truly understood it. Once we worked out the secrets of fire, or combustion, we could create hotter fires, keep them burning for longer, and more easily put them out. And we could use them to power machinery that would change the world.

Up until the mid-1700s, the most popular theory about how fire worked was that it came from a substance called phlogiston, found in wood and other fuels. Then, in 1772, the French chemist Antoine Lavoisier noticed something that would spark off a new theory. He found that the ashes left over from burned materials were heavier than the materials had been. He guessed that the materials had combined with the air. People began to think of fire as a chemical reaction between fuel and oxygen in the air.

A flame would soon go out when the air was pumped out of the container.

Heat, light, and gases, such as carbon dioxide, are created during combustion. We now know that these gases can cause global warming.

The internal combustion engine was invented in the 1790s. The engine used the expanding gases created by combustion to move parts, which could get machines working. In the 1800s, combustion engines powered machinery in mills that made cotton and other goods. Cities grew as people flocked to work in the mills, and they often travelled there on newly invented trains, powered by combustion engines.

Coal-powered machines that created electricity were invented in the 1880s. Today, combustion engines are used in many vehicles, and to make electricity to power our world.

New experiments

During the 1600s, scientists began to experiment with air pumps, which pumped the air from a container. It was found that a candle inside the container would go out. Scientists began to suspect that air played a part in combustion.

WATER VAPOUR

CO2

OXYGEN

FUEL

The secrets of combustion

Fire needs fuel, oxygen, and heat. It is a chemical reaction between the fuel and the oxygen. Many fuels, including wood and oil, contain the element carbon. Combustion releases smoke – a gas, such as carbon dioxide (CO_2), mixed with unburnt fuel particles and water vapour.

Pygmy marmosets are a species in the monkey family.

KINGDOM

One of the largest groups that living things can be categorized into is a kingdom. There are five main kingdoms, including animals (such as the ones shown here), plants, and fungi.

Penguin

Octopus

Crab

Millipede

Geckos belong to the lizard group.

MYSTERY ANIMALS

Some animals have features from multiple species, which makes it hard to put them into a group. The Sunda flying lemur (pictured) stumped scientists because it has skin flaps connected to its hands and feet, like a bat, it climbs trees and has webbed, clawed feet, like a squirrel, and its head is like a lemur's. In the end, it was named a flying lemur – though it is not part of the lemur species!

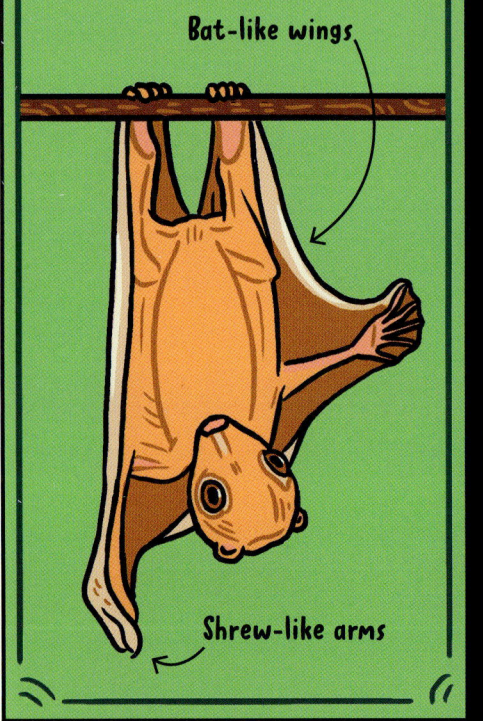

Bat-like wings

Shrew-like arms

SUBPHYLUM

Kingdoms can be split into smaller and smaller groups, such as subphylums. One subphylum of the animal kingdom is "vertebrate", which includes animals with a spine. Animals without a spine are "invertebrates".

Backbone

SPECIES

Subphylums can be divided into species. Penguins are a species of vertebrate. Emperor penguins, such as this one, have thick layers of feathers to keep them warm in the freezing temperatures of their Antarctic home.

Moths are invertebrates.

TAXONOMY

Elf owls are a type of bird.

Creating categories for animals and plants helped us to understand them in new ways.

Today we understand that living things belong to large groups, such as animals and plants, and smaller family groups, such as owls. But it wasn't always that way.

Taxonomy is the grouping, or classification, of living things. People reading this (including you) are all mammals. You are a mammal because you are warm-blooded, were nursed with milk when you were a baby, you grow hair, and you have a spine (though not all creatures with a spine are mammals).

Animals are grouped according to traits that they share. When a new animal is discovered, scientists can use their knowledge of taxonomy to work out if it is part of an existing group.

The creation of today's taxonomy categories is largely thanks to one man, Carl Linnaeus. Born in Sweden in 1707, Linnaeus not only grouped together thousands of plants and animals in his book, *Systema Naturae*, but he came up with a two-part naming system still used today. First comes the category of species (or genus), and then a category within that, called the subcategory. So, he called humans "Homo sapiens" – the genus being "Homo" and the subgroup, "sapiens".

What came next?

Animal knowledge

In order to group animals together, scientists first need to study them. This has led us to learn much more about the animal kingdom – including that marsupials, such as kangaroos, keep their babies in skin pouches, that most lizards lay eggs, and that male seahorses give birth!

Counting animals

It's important to count animals so that we can take steps to protect them if their numbers are falling. Being able to classify animals is the first step to counting how many of a species exist. There are only 100 Amur leopards left in the wild – but many people are working to save them.

Protecting wildlife

Classifying the animals in an area helps us to tell when a species is brought by humans from elsewhere. New species can compete with local wildlife for food. The arrival of the grey squirrel in the UK from the 1890s led to far fewer native red squirrels.

THE ATOM

Everything in the universe is made up of these tiny particles.

In around 400 BCE, Greek philosopher Democritus first wrote that matter is made up of particles – atoms that cannot be divided into anything smaller. But the theory was mostly ignored down the centuries. Finally, the English scientist John Dalton wrote about his new theory of atoms in 1808.

Dalton suggested that the atoms of different elements had different masses. Towards the end of the 1800s, this theory was taken a step further by the scientist J.J. Thomson, when he noticed the existence of a smaller particle than the atom, which he called the electron, in 1897. He thought that atoms must be made up of these smaller, or subatomic, electrons, held together loosely inside a sphere of electrical charge, like fruit dotted through a plum pudding. But the truth was still yet to be discovered. In 1911, New Zealand scientist Ernest Rutherford conducted experiments in which he fired subatomic particles at atoms, expecting them to pass through the empty spaces between the electrons inside. Instead, some particles bounced off something in the centre of the atom. He called this the nucleus. A correct model of the atom was made – with a nucleus at the centre and electrons around the outside.

Protons and neutrons, which make up the atom's nucleus, were discovered in the next few decades. Our knowledge of the atom was now complete. Well, until we found out about gluons, quarks, and the many other subatomic particles.

Electron

Path of electron around the nucleus

ATOM

NUCLEUS

Proton

Ernest Rutherford's laboratory

Quarks and gluons

Quarks are subatomic particles that combine to make neutrons and protons. Gluons hold them together. There are six types of quarks, including up quarks and down quarks. Two up quarks and a down quark form a proton, and two down quarks and an up quark form a neutron.

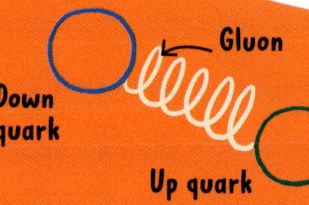

Gluon

Down quark

Up quark

What came next?

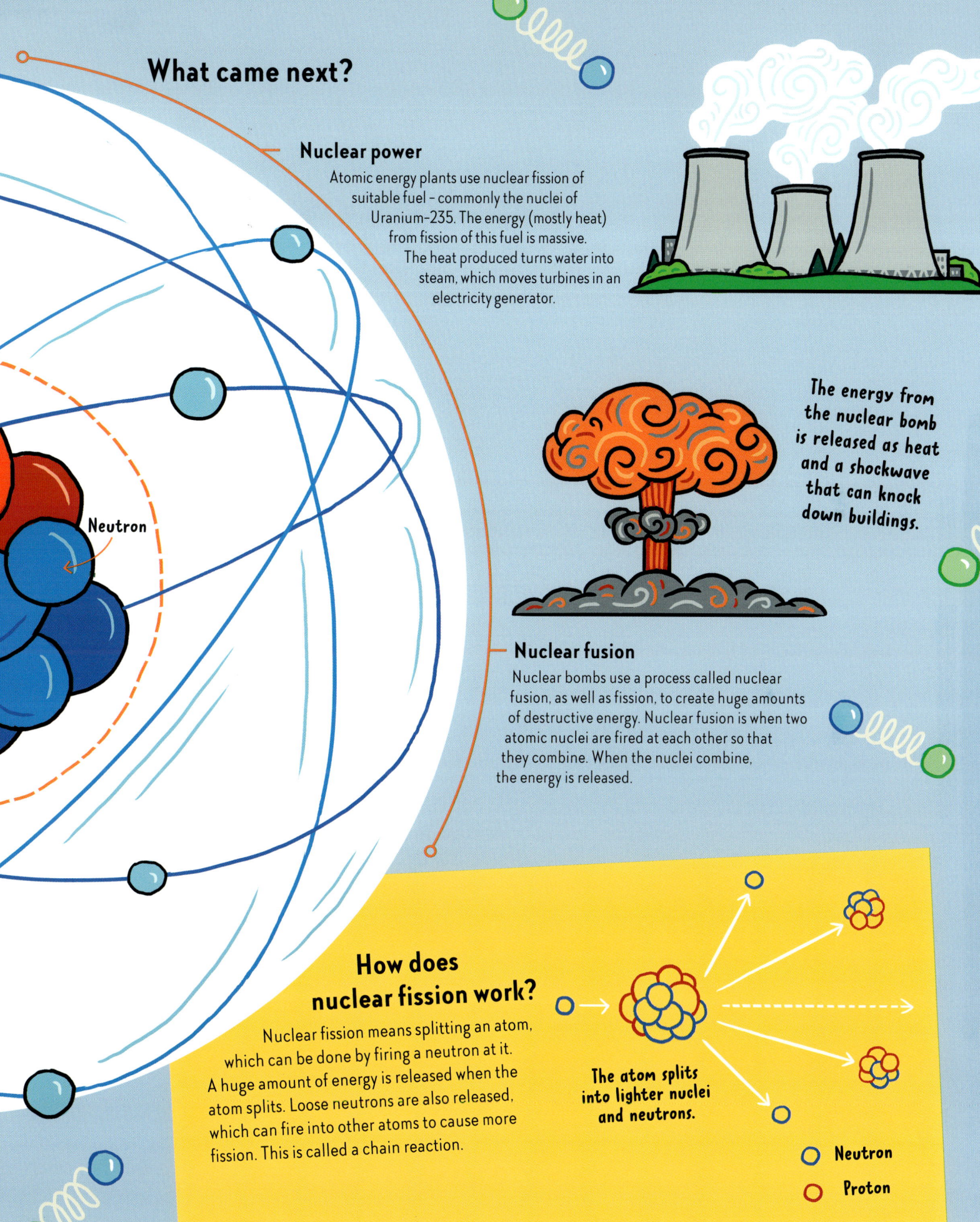

Nuclear power

Atomic energy plants use nuclear fission of suitable fuel – commonly the nuclei of Uranium-235. The energy (mostly heat) from fission of this fuel is massive. The heat produced turns water into steam, which moves turbines in an electricity generator.

Neutron

The energy from the nuclear bomb is released as heat and a shockwave that can knock down buildings.

Nuclear fusion

Nuclear bombs use a process called nuclear fusion, as well as fission, to create huge amounts of destructive energy. Nuclear fusion is when two atomic nuclei are fired at each other so that they combine. When the nuclei combine, the energy is released.

How does nuclear fission work?

Nuclear fission means splitting an atom, which can be done by firing a neutron at it. A huge amount of energy is released when the atom splits. Loose neutrons are also released, which can fire into other atoms to cause more fission. This is called a chain reaction.

The atom splits into lighter nuclei and neutrons.

○ Neutron
○ Proton

45

Ancient evidence

Scientists have found proof of evolution in the form of fossils. These old remains show slightly different versions of animals through time. The horse can be traced back to a cat-sized animal, called Hyracotherium, that lived 55 million years ago.

HYRACOTHERIUM

MESOHIPPUS

MERYCHIPPUS

PLIOHIPPUS

MODERN HORSE

EVOLUTION

In the 1800s, a book was published that changed how people thought about living things.

Throughout history, most people believed that living things, and especially humans, first appeared on the Earth exactly as they were in modern times. But by the 1800s some scientists had begun to question whether living things had changed, or evolved, over time.

When he was 22, the English naturalist Charles Darwin set sail on a five-year trip to study the animals and plants of South America. He noticed that birds from the same species, called finches, had different beaks, depending on which island they lived on, or if they lived on the mainland. Some had wide beaks and some had pointy ones. Perhaps, he thought, they had evolved from the same bird so that they could better survive in new places.

What giraffes tell us

One example that Darwin gave of natural selection was a giraffe's long neck. His theory was that long necks allow these animals to eat leaves off the tops of trees. So, over time, the giraffes with the longest necks survived and passed on their characteristic to young.

Giraffes once had shorter necks, but sometimes a giraffe with a slightly longer neck would be born.

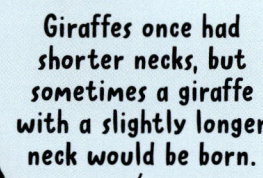

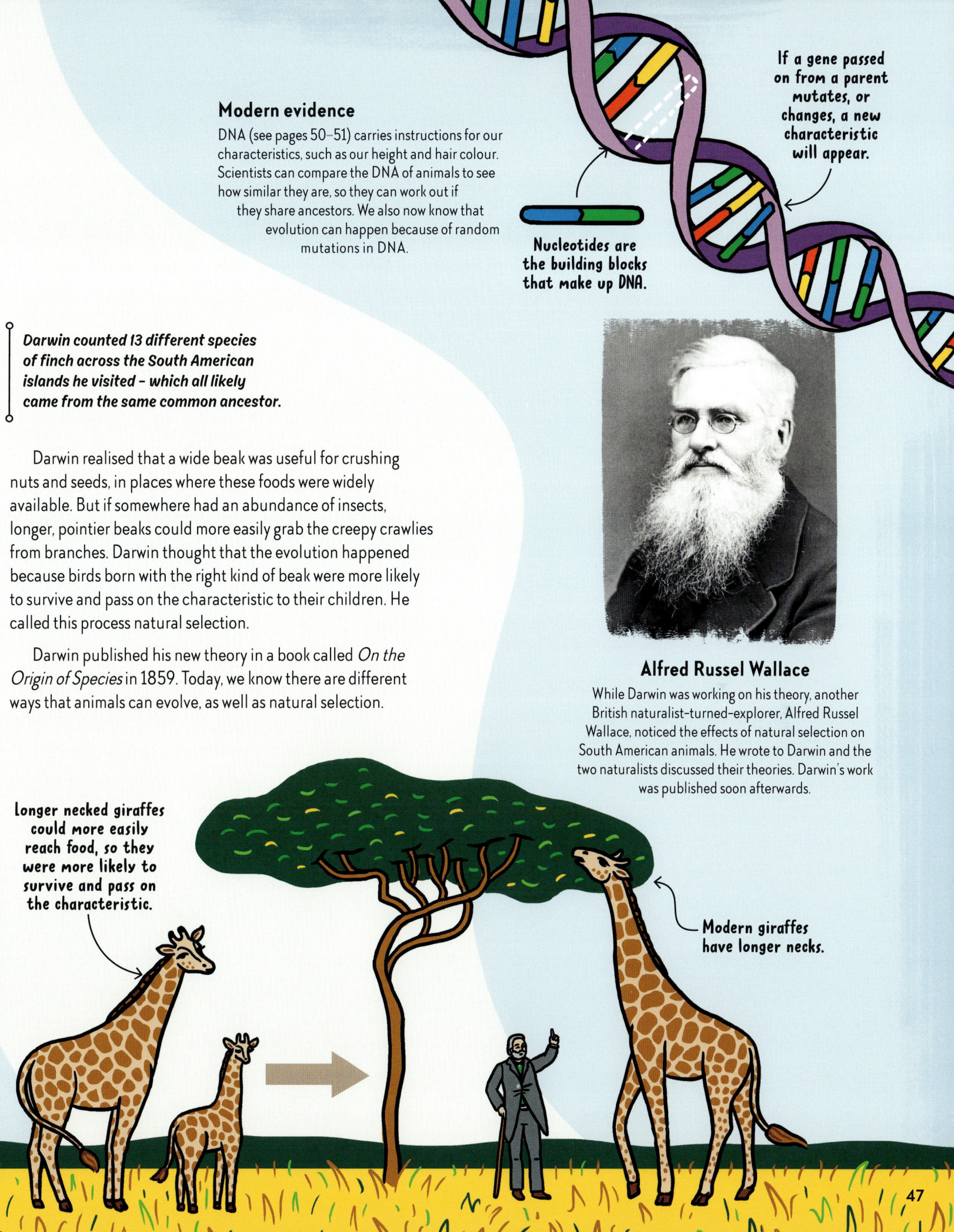

Modern evidence

DNA (see pages 50–51) carries instructions for our characteristics, such as our height and hair colour. Scientists can compare the DNA of animals to see how similar they are, so they can work out if they share ancestors. We also now know that evolution can happen because of random mutations in DNA.

If a gene passed on from a parent mutates, or changes, a new characteristic will appear.

Nucleotides are the building blocks that make up DNA.

Darwin counted 13 different species of finch across the South American islands he visited – which all likely came from the same common ancestor.

Darwin realised that a wide beak was useful for crushing nuts and seeds, in places where these foods were widely available. But if somewhere had an abundance of insects, longer, pointier beaks could more easily grab the creepy crawlies from branches. Darwin thought that the evolution happened because birds born with the right kind of beak were more likely to survive and pass on the characteristic to their children. He called this process natural selection.

Darwin published his new theory in a book called *On the Origin of Species* in 1859. Today, we know there are different ways that animals can evolve, as well as natural selection.

Alfred Russel Wallace

While Darwin was working on his theory, another British naturalist-turned-explorer, Alfred Russel Wallace, noticed the effects of natural selection on South American animals. He wrote to Darwin and the two naturalists discussed their theories. Darwin's work was published soon afterwards.

Longer necked giraffes could more easily reach food, so they were more likely to survive and pass on the characteristic.

Modern giraffes have longer necks.

X-rays

In 1896, Wilhelm Röntgen experimented with a glass apparatus called a Crookes tube. It contained two separated electrodes connected to an electrical source. When Röntgen applied high voltages, invisible energy crossed the space between the electrodes, even when they were separated by black paper. Röntgen had discovered x-rays.

IONISING RADIATION

In the late 1800s, a new, mysterious type of radiation was discovered.

Radiation is energy that travels from a source, such as the Sun or a light bulb, and affects the matter it comes into contact with. It can take various forms, including sound, heat, visible light, infrared and ultraviolet.

Radiation usually transmits in waves, or occasionally in atomic particles. This spread of energy produces an electric and a magnetic field – hence the term, electromagnetic radiation. Microwaves, for example, use radiation to heat up food. With the exception of sound, most radiation can travel in a vacuum and at the speed of light.

Becquerel's uranium rays

Physicist Henri Becquerel was interested in phosphorescent uranium salts. He thought they glowed and left an imprint on photographic paper as a result of absorbing sunlight. During a sunless February, he stored his materials in a dark drawer only to discover that the salts still made an image on the paper. Becquerel had discovered that uranium emits radiation on its own.

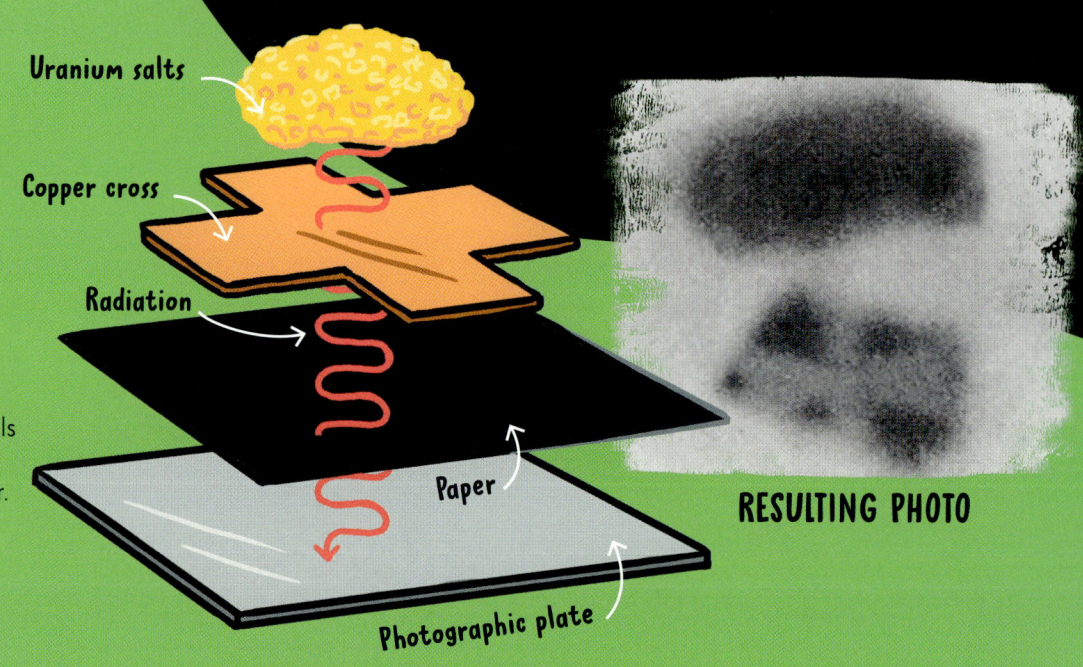

Uranium salts

Copper cross

Radiation

Paper

Photographic plate

RESULTING PHOTO

48

Discovering radium

Husband-and-wife scientists Pierre and Marie Curie explored whether other materials, apart from uranium, emitted radiation naturally. The Curies tested samples using instruments designed by Pierre. The exceptionally heavy work took three years. After shovelling tons of the uranium ore, pitchblende, they isolated one-tenth of a gram of a previously unknown element, radium.

Radium

Pitchblende ore

In the late 1800s, a new, mysterious type of radiation was discovered. This is now called ionising radiation, because it displaces electrons from their atoms, turning the atoms into ions. X-rays are an example of ionising radiation. They are powerful enough to pass through objects, such as books and human tissue.

Ionising radiation is one of medicine's most cutting-edge tools. It allows doctors to see what's going on inside the body, and to destroy diseased cells if necessary.

A dangerous discovery

Ionising radiation can damage living cells, tissue, and DNA. Today, people wear protective clothing if they are exposed to it often. However, scientists did not know about the dangers when they first discovered radiation. Marie Curie sadly died from cancer, which was probably caused by her prolonged exposure to radiation.

Marie Curie's notebooks became radioactive because of how close they were to radium and polonium.

FIRST X-RAY IMAGE

DNA

The structure of this molecule was one of science's great secrets.

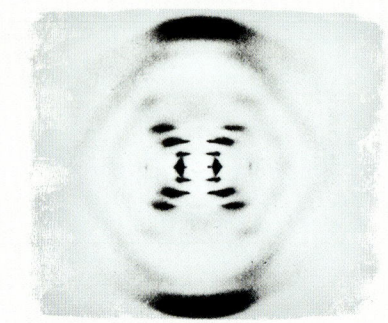

ROSALIND'S WORK
One of the scientists whose work helped Crick and Watson was Rosalind Franklin. A member of her laboratory team took a photo of DNA that showed its shape.

The molecule DNA (deoxyribonucleic acid) sits at the heart of every cell in your body. It contains instructions for every part of you, from the colour of your hair to the size of your heart. The molecule has been known about since the 1860s, but the details of its structure remained a mystery for many years.

It wasn't until 1953 that a scientific duo – James Watson from the USA and Francis Crick from England – discovered DNA's twisted, two-strand structure, called a double helix. The two men put together clues discovered by many other scientists to build a ramshackle model of DNA.

There is hardly a science that is not influenced by this discovery. Scientists study human DNA to work out how diseases might be passed on between people, and how those illnesses might be fixed. Studying the DNA of plants has helped us to find and reproduce crops that are immune to disease. Scientists have even learned how the human species evolved over time by comparing the DNA from modern and ancient people.

Proteins are the building blocks of the body, and DNA carries their instructions. Knowing the structure of DNA led to great advances in the study of proteins – called molecular biology.

How it works

The body is made up of different types of cells, which join to form different parts of the body. The heart of each cell is called the nucleus, and inside the nucleus sit genes, or chromosomes, made of DNA. Humans usually have 46 chromosomes, joined into 23 pairs. Each pair contains a chromosome from the mother and one from the father.

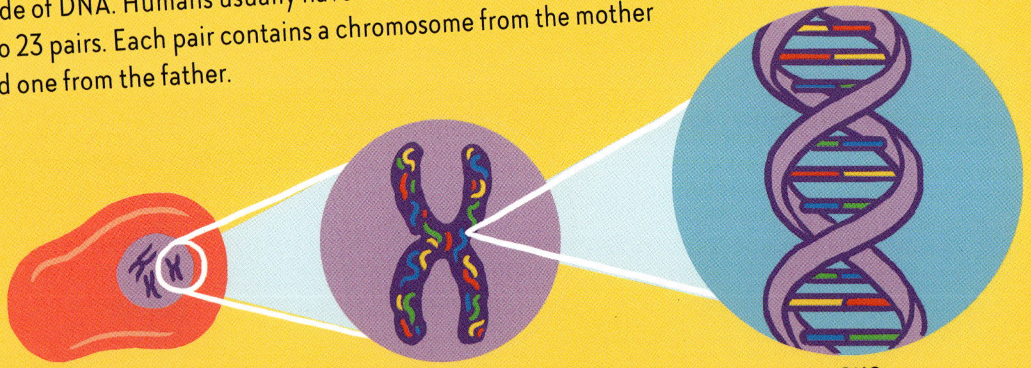

Body cell

Chromosome

DNA

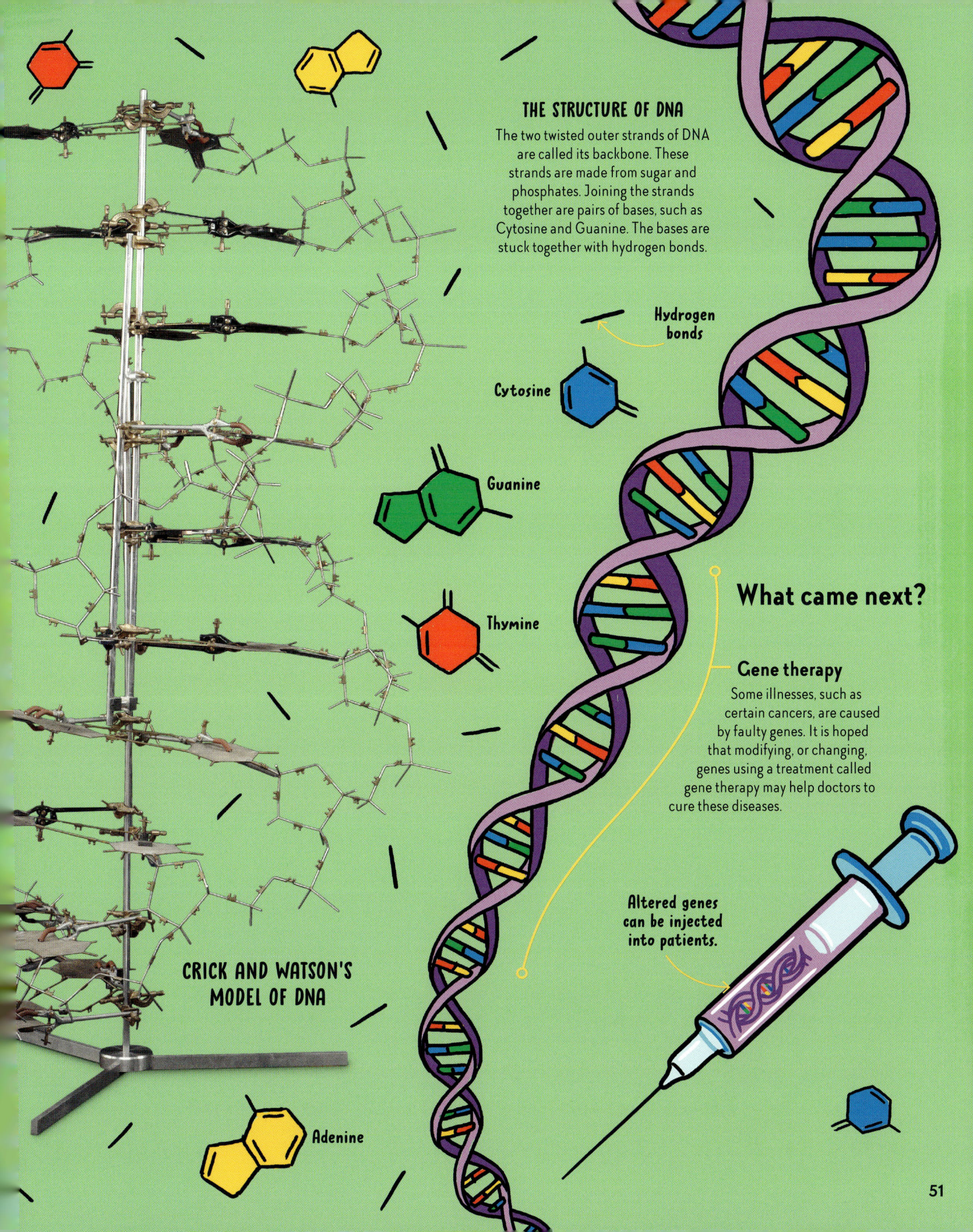

THE STRUCTURE OF DNA

The two twisted outer strands of DNA are called its backbone. These strands are made from sugar and phosphates. Joining the strands together are pairs of bases, such as Cytosine and Guanine. The bases are stuck together with hydrogen bonds.

Hydrogen bonds

Cytosine

Guanine

Thymine

Adenine

CRICK AND WATSON'S MODEL OF DNA

What came next?

Gene therapy

Some illnesses, such as certain cancers, are caused by faulty genes. It is hoped that modifying, or changing, genes using a treatment called gene therapy may help doctors to cure these diseases.

Altered genes can be injected into patients.

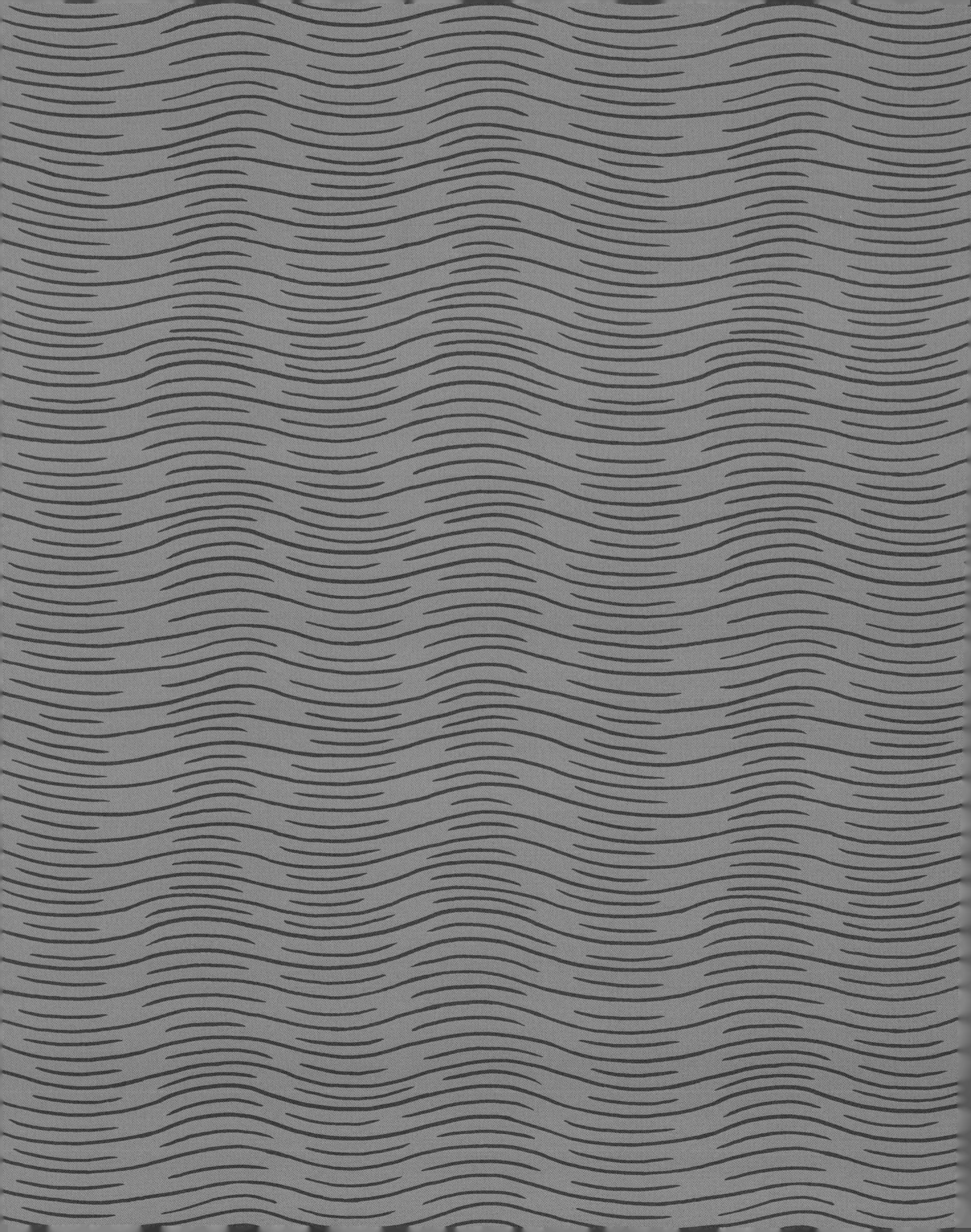

CHAPTER 4

TRANSPORTATION

All methods of transport have benefited from scientific progress. Science tells us which materials to use when making vehicles, how to make vehicles go, and more.

The earliest wheels, made thousands of years ago, were carved from solid wood. Now, we know that materials with less mass go faster, and so we use different materials for wheels. Engineers know that they need to build planes that won't be affected by air resistance, which could slow them down. Racing cars can go fastest on wheels with smooth tyres, which will rub less against the road and create less friction. But smoother tyres make it harder to grip the road when steering. Modern transportation also requires calculation. The thrust of an engine, which makes a vehicle go, needs to be more powerful for vehicles with more mass. Power to weight ratio is also critically important when trying to leave Earth's gravitational field to go into space.

BOATS

Although primitive paddle and rowing boats existed for many years before, the earliest historical evidence of sailboats can be found in pictures from ancient Egypt that were made in roughly 4000 BCE.

CHARIOT

The earliest chariots are thought to have been invented in Mesopotamia around 3000 BCE. However, the oldest confirmed ones date back to 2000 BCE. The Romans used horse-drawn chariots for sports, entertainment, and to transport materials and goods.

4000 BCE

2000 BCE

1555

THE HISTORY OF TRANSPORTATION

Humans have been creating different modes of transport for thousands of years, many of which were developed in line with industrial and technological improvements. Here are just some of the many crucial milestones in the history of transportation.

HORSE AND CARRIAGE

Carriages drawn by two or four horses were introduced in England in around 1555. Only royalty and the very rich could afford them but the roads were bumpy and it would have been an unpleasant ride!

1825

FIRST PASSENGER TRAIN

The world's first public railway journey took place in Durham, England in 1825 on a steam engine called Locomotion No.1. It had a top speed of 25kph (15mph).

FIRST UNDERGROUND RAILWAY

On 10th January 1863, the world's first underground railway opened in London.

1863

AUTOMOBILE

In 1886, in what is considered the birth of the automobile, Karl Benz patented his 'vehicle powered by a gas engine'. However, Henry Ford's Model T, introduced in 1908, is credited with being the first mass market vehicle for the public.

1886

BUSES

In an attempt to make to make automobile technology more accessible to the public, Karl Benz invented the first motorized bus. It went into service in 1895, with space for eight people, including the driver.

1895

1881

TRAM/STREETCAR

The first electrically operated streetcar was invented by Werner von Siemens in Berlin in 1881. It was a great success, and transported 12,000 passengers in its first three months.

AEROPLANE

The first fuel-powered controlled flight was achieved by the Wright Brothers in 1903. Just over a decade later, in 1914, the first commercial passenger flight took off from Florida, USA on New Year's Day.

1903

PETROL SCOOTER

Arthur Gibson patented a petrol propelled scooter called 'the Autoped', which was popular with suffragettes in 1916. The machine was expensive and it weighed nearly 100kg (220lb). It failed to sell and became a flop.

1916

BICYCLE

The Penny-farthing, also known as the high-wheeler, was introduced in 1869. It was arguably the first true bicycle.

1869

What came next?

Until recent years, speed and comfort were selling points. Now, we focus more on safety and on reducing pollution.

Hybrid and electric cars

Hybrid cars have more than one power source – usually a combination of a petrol engine and an electric motor. But cars that are solely powered with electricity are becoming increasingly common as battery technology improves.

E-bikes

Pedal bicycles are an environmentally friendly method of transportation. E-bikes have an electric motor to assist the rider pedalling. Roads or lanes just for bicyclists help to keep them safe from other vehicles.

SAILBOATS

From early fishing boats and warships, to merchant clippers and sleek pleasure yachts, boats and their sails have evolved over thousands of years. Using the power of the wind, sailboats have enabled humans to explore, conquer, trade, and travel.

MESOPOTAMIAN REED BOAT

Possibly the first ever sailboats, they could sail close to shore and were probably used mainly for fishing. The crab-claw sail edged with poles (pictured) could be lowered for safety in high winds, though the stiff poles were difficult to handle.

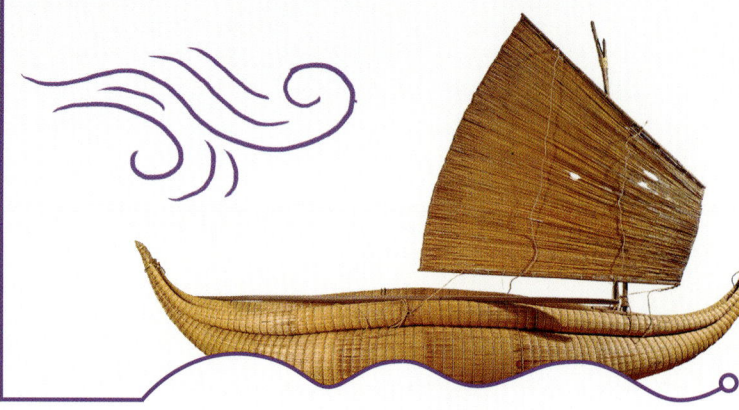

GALLEY SHIP

Galleys were armed warships that were powered by rowing oarsmen. If the wind blew favourably, they sometimes used sails to gain speed. Unlike sailboats that could only move in the direction of the wind, galleys could go anywhere their captain wanted.

LONGBOAT

Longboats were often carried or towed by a mother ship to ferry the captain or crew to shore, or to carry provisions, such as food or weapons. Occasionally, longboats were sent to rescue careless sailors who, if they were lucky, survived falling overboard.

CHINESE JUNK SHIP

Chinese builders made advanced, wooden, seagoing ships with multiple decks, strong bulkheads and watertight compartments well before the Europeans. Eyewitness accounts suggest that some junks carried up to 400 soldiers and even more crew.

SPANISH GALLEON

The design of Spanish galleon ships influenced international ship-building for centuries. Galleons were built for stability, powered entirely by their sails, and were armed with cannons on both sides. In 1588, the king of Spain ordered a huge fleet of galleons, known as the Spanish Armada, to invade England. It failed.

YACHT

Yachts are primarily sailed for fun. King James I of England gave his son a yacht as a present, and it was the first time a royal ship was used for leisure. The first yacht race took place in 1661. Yachts are generally more than 10 m (33 ft) long, have sails or engines, and facilities for sleeping and cooking.

DUTCH FLUYT

Fluyts were fairly similar to galleon ships, but built for transporting cargo, not soldiers. With a flat bottom, they could navigate shallow Dutch waters, docking easily in small ports. Fluyts needed fewer crew members than armed ships.

CLIPPER

Clippers were built to bring tea from China to Europe and North America, from about 1850. Slim and long with a huge sail area, the *Cutty Sark* was possibly the fastest clipper, travelling at 20 knots – even beating steam-powered liners going flat out.

CATAMARAN

Catamarans originated in Pacific Australasia. With two parallel hulls, they are buoyant and displace less water than single-hulled ships. They are stable sailing boats, but when powered by engines they can provide rapid transport through inland lakes and waterways.

THE WHEEL

Humans were on a roll from the day they invented this.

It is hard to know when wheels were first invented, as they were likely made from wood that has rotted away over time. Early wheels that have survived date back thousands of years and were used for simple machines.

The first type of wheel is thought to have been a pottery wheel, made to spin clay so that it could easily be shaped into pots from around 3500 BCE. The earliest known cartwheel dates back to around 3350 BCE. With the invention of carts came the ability to move huge amounts of stone to build the great monuments of the past.

Wheels turn on a pole called an axle. Early wheels would have rubbed on their wooden axle, causing friction to slow the wheels. Slippery substances, such as fat, were found to stop rubbing.

Over time, many more inventions were made with wheels at their centre. From around 300 BCE, wheels set in motion by moving water turned machinery to grind grains into flour. Spinning wheels were invented to turn cotton into thread for making clothes. Eventually, we invented propellers that could spin fast enough to lift helicopters and planes into the air.

STONE WHEEL

The first pottery wheels were used in Sumer, in what is now Iraq.

What came next?

Wheelbarrows

Chinese illustrations from 2,000 years ago show people using wheelbarrows. This clever machine allows a person to carry a load much heavier than what they could hold in their arms. This is because the weight of the load rests partly on the wheel of the barrow.

Motor cars

The first cars were invented in the late 1800s and used bicycle-like wheels – narrow, with hard rubber around the outside. These tyres did not cushion drivers from the bumps of the road, but they allowed them to travel directly and quickly from one place to the next.

Modern tyres

Today, bicycles, cars, lorries, and other vehicles use rubber tyres filled with air to cushion the vehicle from bumps in the road. Grooves around the outside help the tyres to grip icy or wet roads. Vehicles designed to travel offroad have deeper grooves so that they don't slip in mud.

How did wheels improve over time?

The first wheels were carved from solid wood. The wheels were heavy and slow to turn, and they could only be as wide as the tree trunk from which they were carved. Later, people used wooden planks to make bigger wheels, and they added gaps into the structure to make lighter wheels.

Solid wheels were cut from logs.

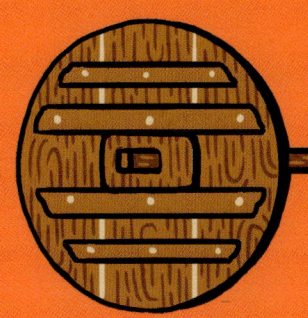

Plank wheels were made from planks held together by crosspieces.

Spoke

Crossbar wheels had a crossbar across the middle and spokes.

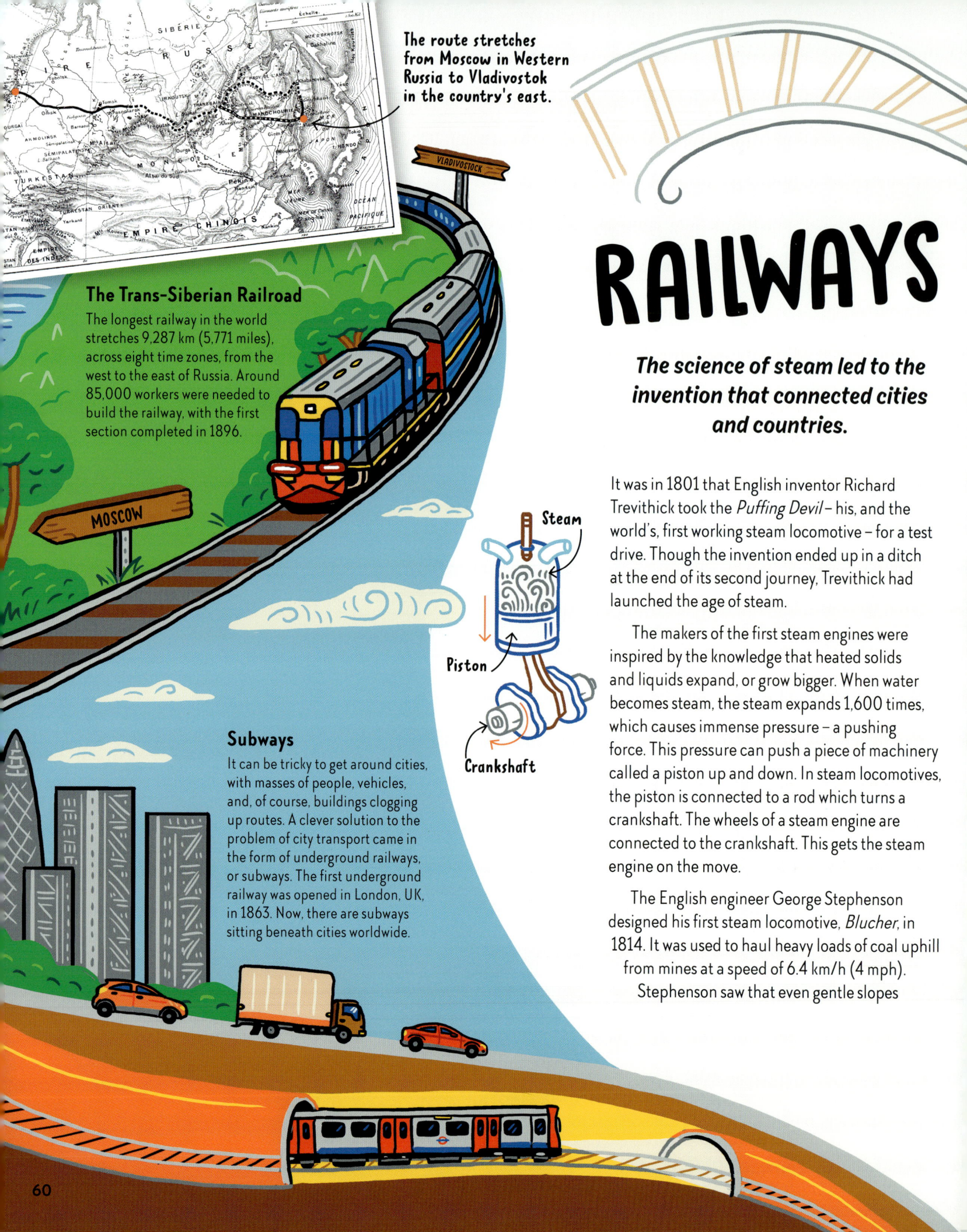

The route stretches from Moscow in Western Russia to Vladivostok in the country's east.

VLADIVOSTOCK

The Trans-Siberian Railroad

The longest railway in the world stretches 9,287 km (5,771 miles), across eight time zones, from the west to the east of Russia. Around 85,000 workers were needed to build the railway, with the first section completed in 1896.

MOSCOW

Subways

It can be tricky to get around cities, with masses of people, vehicles, and, of course, buildings clogging up routes. A clever solution to the problem of city transport came in the form of underground railways, or subways. The first underground railway was opened in London, UK, in 1863. Now, there are subways sitting beneath cities worldwide.

Steam

Piston

Crankshaft

RAILWAYS

The science of steam led to the invention that connected cities and countries.

It was in 1801 that English inventor Richard Trevithick took the *Puffing Devil* – his, and the world's, first working steam locomotive – for a test drive. Though the invention ended up in a ditch at the end of its second journey, Trevithick had launched the age of steam.

The makers of the first steam engines were inspired by the knowledge that heated solids and liquids expand, or grow bigger. When water becomes steam, the steam expands 1,600 times, which causes immense pressure – a pushing force. This pressure can push a piece of machinery called a piston up and down. In steam locomotives, the piston is connected to a rod which turns a crankshaft. The wheels of a steam engine are connected to the crankshaft. This gets the steam engine on the move.

The English engineer George Stephenson designed his first steam locomotive, *Blucher*, in 1814. It was used to haul heavy loads of coal uphill from mines at a speed of 6.4 km/h (4 mph). Stephenson saw that even gentle slopes

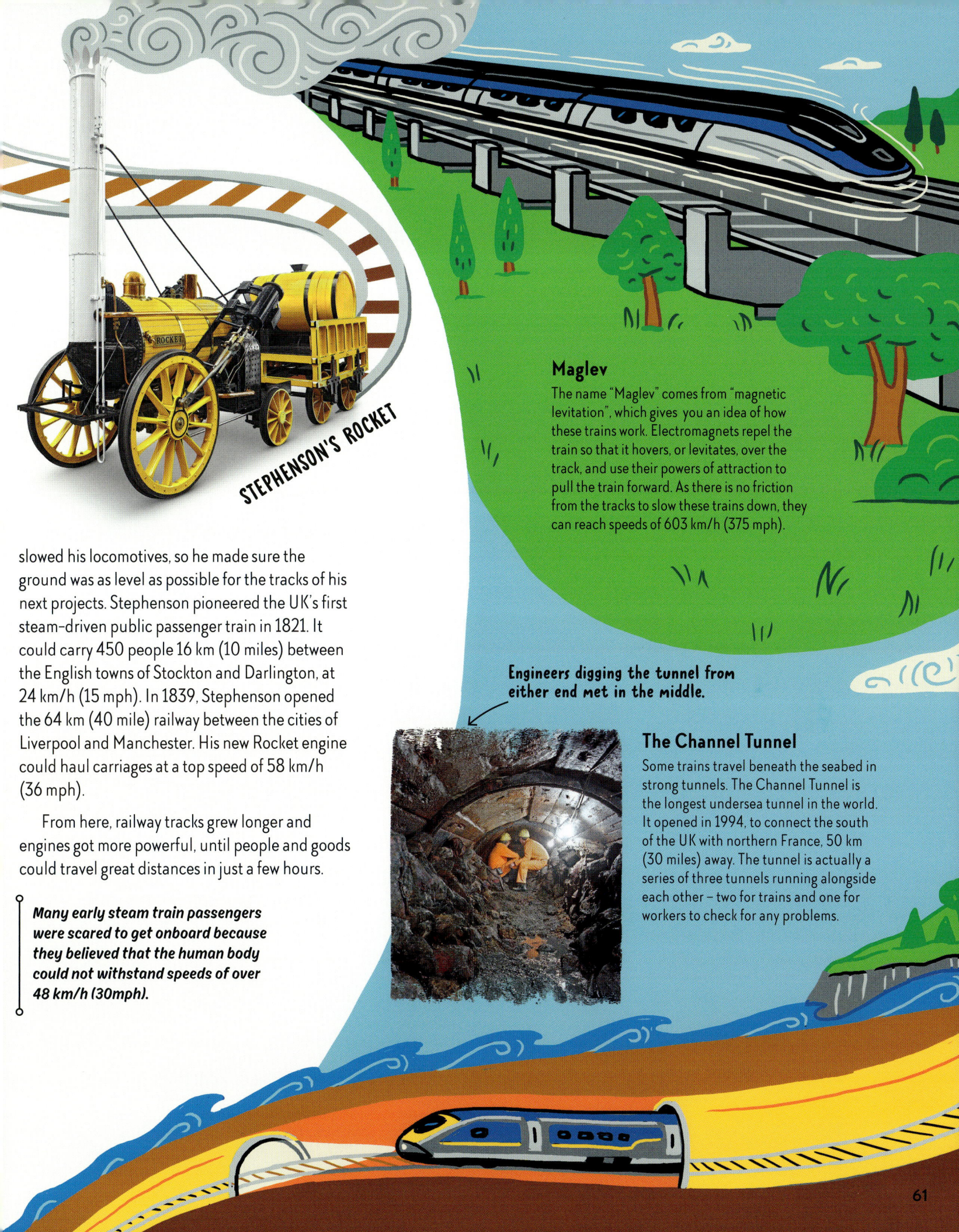

STEPHENSON'S ROCKET

Maglev

The name "Maglev" comes from "magnetic levitation", which gives you an idea of how these trains work. Electromagnets repel the train so that it hovers, or levitates, over the track, and use their powers of attraction to pull the train forward. As there is no friction from the tracks to slow these trains down, they can reach speeds of 603 km/h (375 mph).

slowed his locomotives, so he made sure the ground was as level as possible for the tracks of his next projects. Stephenson pioneered the UK's first steam-driven public passenger train in 1821. It could carry 450 people 16 km (10 miles) between the English towns of Stockton and Darlington, at 24 km/h (15 mph). In 1839, Stephenson opened the 64 km (40 mile) railway between the cities of Liverpool and Manchester. His new Rocket engine could haul carriages at a top speed of 58 km/h (36 mph).

From here, railway tracks grew longer and engines got more powerful, until people and goods could travel great distances in just a few hours.

Many early steam train passengers were scared to get onboard because they believed that the human body could not withstand speeds of over 48 km/h (30mph).

Engineers digging the tunnel from either end met in the middle.

The Channel Tunnel

Some trains travel beneath the seabed in strong tunnels. The Channel Tunnel is the longest undersea tunnel in the world. It opened in 1994, to connect the south of the UK with northern France, 50 km (30 miles) away. The tunnel is actually a series of three tunnels running alongside each other – two for trains and one for workers to check for any problems.

BIPLANE

The first ever working airplane, flown by the Wright brothers, had two stacked wings for better lift. But biplanes were quite slow, and after World War II, airplanes with just one wing on either side became the standard.

AVIATION

Humans have always been enchanted by the idea of flying. Some even experimented by jumping off cliffs with homemade wings. As science and technology developed, flight became possible, achievable, and – eventually – available to the masses.

JET PLANE

Jet planes are flying machines that are powered by fuel and reach high altitudes. Their streamlined design reduces air resistance and allows them to fly vast distances at high speeds. Nowadays, jet planes are used for commercial travel and have made it possible for people to visit destinations all around the globe.

The first commercial jet was the De Havilland DH-106 Comet I.

MISSILE

Unfortunately, the science of aviation has brought about advances in warfare, too. Rocket-propelled missiles can shoot explosives or biological weapons over long distances. The latest technology allows missiles to be aimed at their targets with incredible precision.

HELICOPTER

Helicopters have horizontal rotating propellors which act like wings and create lift, allowing the aircraft to rise vertically or hover. This gives helicopters the useful ability to take off and land in many more places than winged aircraft can.

FLYING BOAT

Flying boats have floats rather than wheels, which allows them to land on a suitable stretch of water without need of a runway. The floats are bulky, however, which limits their flying speed and can make taking off difficult.

FIGHTER JET

The first fighter jets were designed during World War II. They were created for warfare so they needed to be fast, manoeuvrable, and able to carry weapons. Modern fighter jets can reach speeds of more than 1,600 km (1,000 miles) per hour.

HOT AIR BALLOON

Hot air balloons use heated gas to rise up into the air, so they don't rely on engines or complex machinery to fly. While they are slower than airplanes, using hot air as a power source has its advantages: it is not explosive like hydrogen, flammable like petrol, or expensive like helium.

SPACECRAFT

Rocket propulsion requires huge amounts of energy from combustion to escape Earth's gravity. The first craft to travel to space was *Sputnik 1,* an uncrewed Soviet satellite launched in 1957. In 1969, Neil Armstrong became the first person to set foot on the Moon. NASA's *Voyager 1* has travelled further than any other spacecraft – more than 22 billion km (14 billion miles) from Earth!

The first hot air balloon flight took place in 1783 – 120 years before the Wright brothers flew!

DRONE

Pilotless flying machines, drones are used by the military for reconnaissance. They can also carry weapons. Drone technology is changing and becoming more accessible. It is now possible to buy a small personal drone for taking aerial photos and videos.

Apollo 8 took people to orbit the Moon for the first time.

CHAPTER 5

EXPLORATION

What makes humans want to explore? Of course, we are inquisitive. But we also desire adventure. We feel we must go somewhere that nobody else has ever set foot before.

Throughout history, an excitement at the unknown and the wish to better understand things has driven scientists. But there is something else, too. When we scientists explore, we hope to find ways to improve our world. By understanding, we hope really to do good, often not only for humankind but for the planet and all its living creatures.

You who are reading this book have a great opportunity. You might dream of finding new, wonderful places. But you can also explore the world when you look through a telescope or see the remarkable structures of life and matter under the microscope. And you might even make new scientific discoveries that change our world for the better.

NAVIGATION

From following intricate maps of the stars, to pressing a few buttons on handheld electronic devices, navigation has changed greatly over the last few thousand years. A range of brilliant discoveries and ingenious inventions have given us tools that can tell you exactly where on Earth you are.

ASTROLABE

From around the 8th century, explorers used highly detailed, handheld astrolabes for navigation. They calculated latitude by noting the position of the Sun or stars through holes in the instrument, which was engraved with star maps. Unfortunately, the constantly moving horizon on rocking ships affected the astrolabe's accuracy.

MARINE CHRONOMETER

Sailors were unable to confirm longitude without knowing the local time, and getting lost at sea was tragically common. The marine chronometer, invented in the 18th century, was able to measure time accurately as sea thus giving explorers the final piece of navigational information they needed.

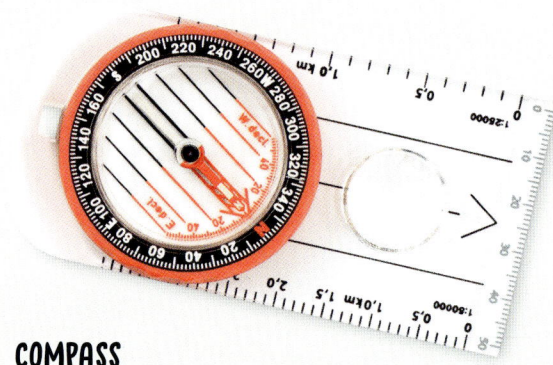

CHART

Cuneiform maps have been found from Babylon and a new discovery is thought to include 25,000-year-old maps carved on mammoth tusks. While these ancient charts show how important navigation was, they are not accurate representations of land or distance.

COMPASS

Two thousand years ago, Chinese inventors used lodestone, a naturally magnetic mineral, as a compass. Suspended on string, they called it the "South Pointing Fish" because the lodestone was magnetically attracted to the South Pole. Eventually, they reversed it to point north, and improved its accuracy by using lodestone to magnetise needles.

Sextants allow sailors to plot their boat's position accurately within 185 metres (200 yards).

SHIP'S LOG

This simple instrument helps sailors track two crucial measurements: speed, and how far they've travelled. The ship's log is a propellor that turns through the water whilst connected to a gauge. By counting the revolutions, it estimates speed and distance.

SEXTANT

Another 18th century invention, the sextant measures the angles and distances between objects in the sky (the Sun, moon, or stars) and the horizon. Though quite technical, sextants are simple to use and are not affected by the ship's motion.

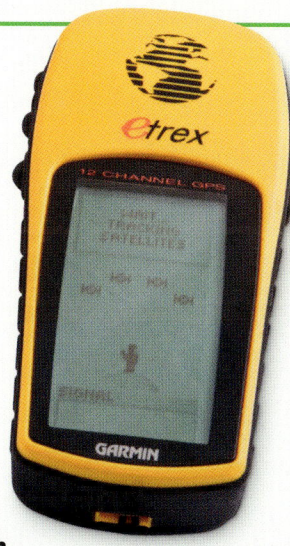

RADAR

Radar uses the reflection of radio waves to detect hidden objects. Developed primarily for military use, radar is now used to guide ships and aircraft safely, and for weather forecasting. If radar had been available in 1912, the Titanic would not have hit that iceberg.

GPS

The Global Positioning System was developed by the USA in the early 1970s and is the most accurate navigational tool we have. There are 24 satellites in orbit 20,000 km (12,500 miles) above Earth. Having four of them above you will give your location within 4 metres (13 ft).

THE COMPASS

This device pointed explorers in the right direction.

Long ago, people navigated using the Sun and stars, which appear in different parts of the sky when viewed from different places. But this type of navigation is impossible in cloudy weather. The magnetic compass, however, can be used at almost any time.

Scientists in China first discovered that they could use magnets to tell where they were in around 300 BCE. If spun, a spoon made of naturally magnetic rock would come to rest with the handle pointing south. From here, every other direction could be discovered. Later, Chinese scientists worked out that an iron needle could be rubbed with magnetic stone to magnetize it, attached to cork so that it floated, and placed in water so that it spun and came to rest with one end pointing north.

From around 1000 CE, smaller compasses with free-moving magnetic needles were used by explorers to discover unknown lands. These devices helped us to map the world.

There were 24 directions for spoon compasses to point towards.

Directions were written around the outside of the compass.

SPOON COMPASS

How does it work?

The Earth has a magnetic field, which means electrically charged particles are drawn in a circular path around it. The field runs through two points at opposite ends of the Earth, called the magnetic north and south. Magnetic materials are affected by the field. So, free-moving compass needles – such as a magnetized needle floating in water – will spin to line up with the field, pointing north and south.

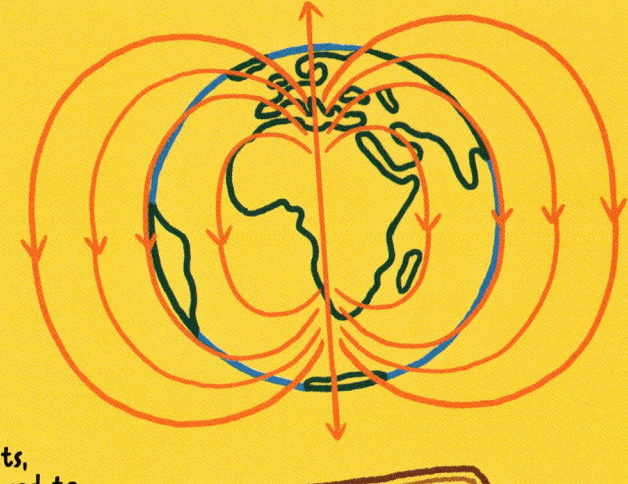

Cork floats, so it can be used to hold the needle up.

The magnetized needle moves freely in the water.

Four main directions are written around the outside of compass needles - north, east, south, and west.

What came next?

True north

Magnetic north

A new north

Compasses point to a magnetic north. But in 1909 the explorer Robert Peary proved that this is not, in fact, the Earth's most northern point – the North Pole. Peary was part of the first expedition to reach the North Pole. Once there, his compass pointed south to a magnetic north 800 km (497 m) away.

GPS

Today, many people use a global positioning system (GPS) to find their way around. GPS receiving devices, such as mobile phones, pick up radio signals from satellites orbiting the Earth. The time it takes for signals from different satellites to reach the device tells it where it is.

THE CHRONOMETER

The longitude of a place describes how far east or west it is of the Prime Meridian line (in red).

An accurate clock was the key to exploring the world.

Sailors once used the time to work out their location, by counting the hours and minutes that had passed since they had sailed east or west from land. But up until the 1700s, clocks could not tell the time at sea accurately. The marine chronometer was a clock designed to work on ships, and it was the result of one man's lifelong determination.

It is very important that seafarers know where they are at sea. This became clear to the British government in 1707, when four Royal Navy ships sank after striking rocks near the Isles of Scilly. The ships might not have sunk if their captains had known exactly where they were, and been able to avoid the rocks. So, the British government decided to offer a £20,000 prize to an inventor who could solve the problem. That's over £3 million in today's money!

An English carpenter, John Harrison, set out to win the prize. He used metals that expanded and contracted at different rates with changes in temperature. He noted that a swinging pendulum was affected by the ship's movement, so he found a different way to count seconds. His first clock was used to accurately work out a ship's position.

John perfected his timepieces over 30 years, until he made a watch that did not lose time when it was wound up. John was never given his prize money, but his name became part of history.

Mapping the world

Maps were often wrong before chronometers were invented. It was hard for sailors to mark down the exact location of an island or coastline. The chronometer changed this. In the 1770s, the British explorer Captain Cooke used his chronometer to make the most accurate map of the Pacific Ocean to date, which was used for the next 200 years.

What came next?

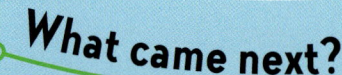

New York   Toyko

Greenwich Mean Time

Time zones

Chronometers on British ships were often set to the time at Greenwich, UK. As Britain colonized countries around the world, the times in these places were set a certain number of hours ahead of or behind Greenwich. In 1844, the world was divided into 24 equally sized time zones.

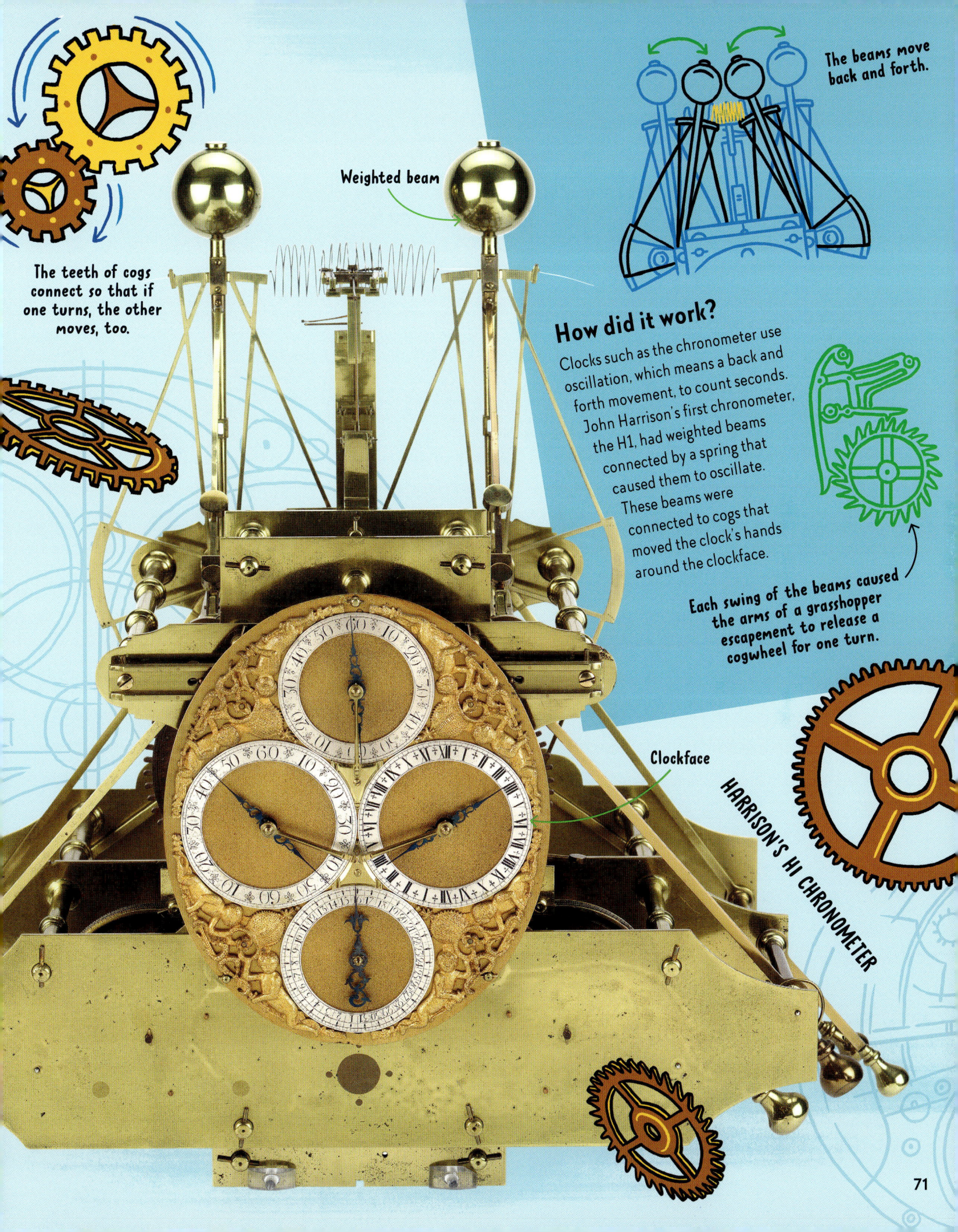

The teeth of cogs connect so that if one turns, the other moves, too.

Weighted beam

The beams move back and forth.

How did it work?

Clocks such as the chronometer use oscillation, which means a back and forth movement, to count seconds. John Harrison's first chronometer, the H1, had weighted beams connected by a spring that caused them to oscillate. These beams were connected to cogs that moved the clock's hands around the clockface.

Each swing of the beams caused the arms of a grasshopper escapement to release a cogwheel for one turn.

Clockface

HARRISON'S H1 CHRONOMETER

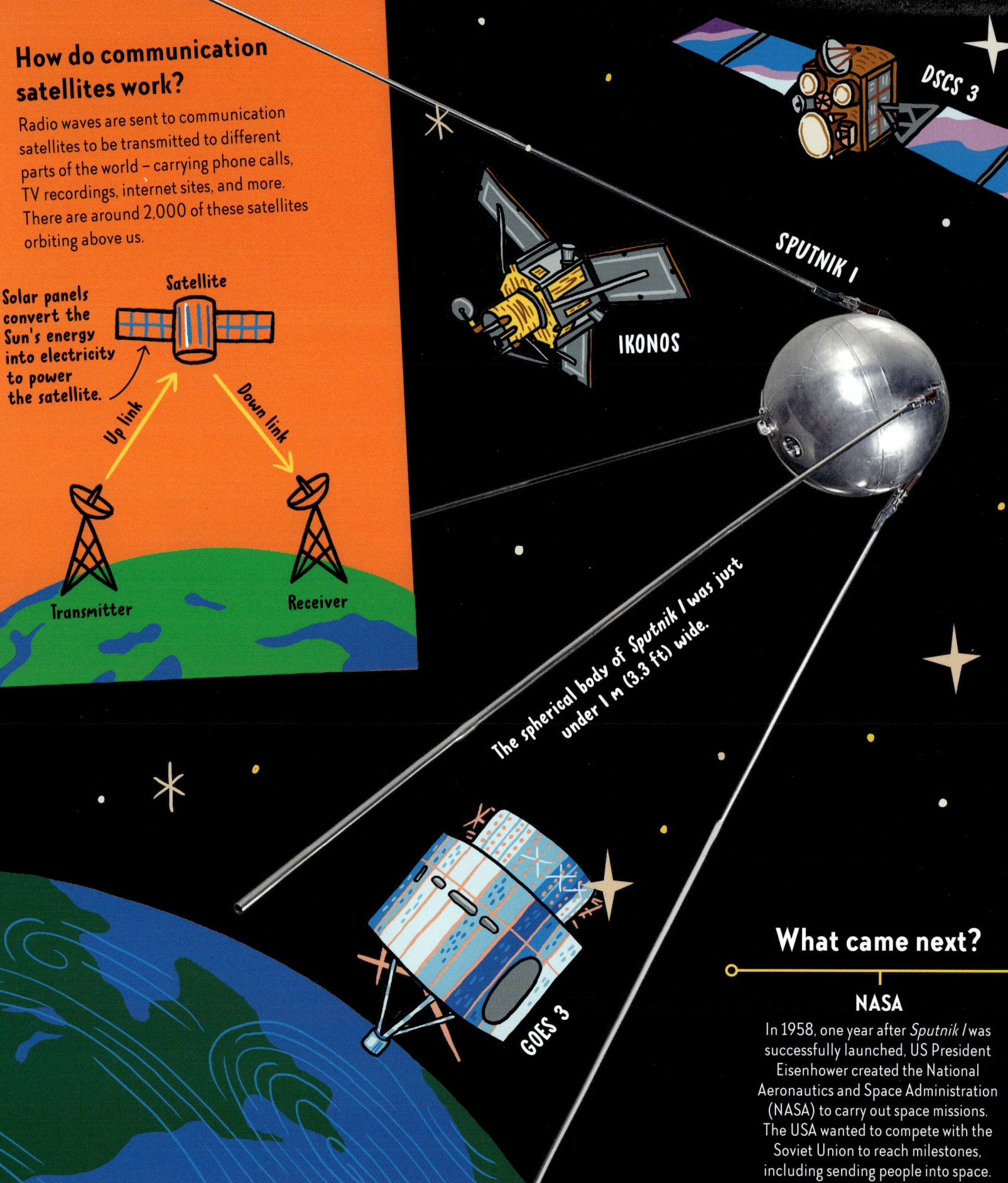

How do communication satellites work?

Radio waves are sent to communication satellites to be transmitted to different parts of the world – carrying phone calls, TV recordings, internet sites, and more. There are around 2,000 of these satellites orbiting above us.

Solar panels convert the Sun's energy into electricity to power the satellite.

Satellite

Up link

Down link

Transmitter

Receiver

DSCS 3

SPUTNIK I

IKONOS

The spherical body of *Sputnik I* was just under 1 m (3.3 ft) wide.

GOES 3

What came next?

NASA

In 1958, one year after *Sputnik I* was successfully launched, US President Eisenhower created the National Aeronautics and Space Administration (NASA) to carry out space missions. The USA wanted to compete with the Soviet Union to reach milestones, including sending people into space.

SATELLITES

These were the first spacecraft in the sky – and thousands orbit above us today.

The famous scientist Isaac Newton first wrote about artificial (human-made) satellites in 1687. He proposed that a giant cannonball fired into space might be pulled into orbit around the Earth by gravity (see pages 38–39). But satellites were merely science fiction until after the Second World War, when rockets that could escape the Earth's gravity were invented.

In 1957 the Soviet Union (now Russia) launched the first artificial satellite, *Sputnik 1*, into orbit. Today, satellites beam TV shows into homes and transfer text messages between mobile phones on opposite ends of the Earth. Satellites monitor the Earth's weather and take photographs – both of our planet and of the wonders of deep space. And, because they are above our atmosphere, satellites are safe from the oxygen and rain that cause other machines to rust.

There now close to 6,000 satellites in the sky. Many are geostationary, which means they orbit in the direction of the Earth's spin and stay above the same spot as the Earth turns.

Starlink satellites, which send internet content, travel in a line across the sky – see if you can spot them one night!

The lunar module of Apollo 11 was called "Eagle".

Moon landing

In 1961, the Soviet Union's Yuri Gagarin became the first person to go into space. The USA were now determined to be the first to reach the Moon. Finally, in 1969, NASA's *Apollo 11* carried Neil Armstrong, Buzz Aldrin, and Michael Collins to the Moon. Armstrong and Aldrin were the first people to set foot on its surface.

Exploration of Mars

The first spacecraft to land on Mars was NASA's *Viking I*, in 1976. It sent back images of the red planet's surface. The *Mars Pathfinder* was the first robotic rover to reach Mars in 1997. It returned huge amounts of data, including the temperature throughout the day and the makeup of the rocks and soil.

SPACE RACE

In 1955, the USA and the Soviet Union began a race to conquer space. First, they strove to send uncrewed spaceships into orbit, and later to land people on the Moon.

THE MERCURY SEVEN
A group of seven people were chosen to be the USA's first astronauts. They flew spacecraft for NASA's first human spaceflight programme, Project Mercury, and for later NASA programmes, such as Apollo.

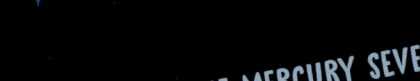

A SATELLITE IN SPACE
The Soviet Union's *Sputnik 1* became the first artificial satellite to reach space. It orbited the Earth more than 1,400 times in three months.

APRIL 9TH 1959

31ST JANUARY 1958

NOVEMBER 3RD 1957

OCTOBER 4TH 1957

THE USA'S FIRST SATELLITE
The USA launched their first satellite, *Explorer 1*, several months after the Soviets.

FIRST SPACE DOG
Laika was a Soviet space dog who became the first animal to orbit the Earth. She flew aboard the *Sputnik 2* spacecraft.

AN AMERICAN DREAM
The USA declared their goal to send an artificial satellite into space.

THE USSR ANSWERS
The USSR announced their own satellite programme. The race had begun.

2ND AUGUST 1955

29TH JULY 1955

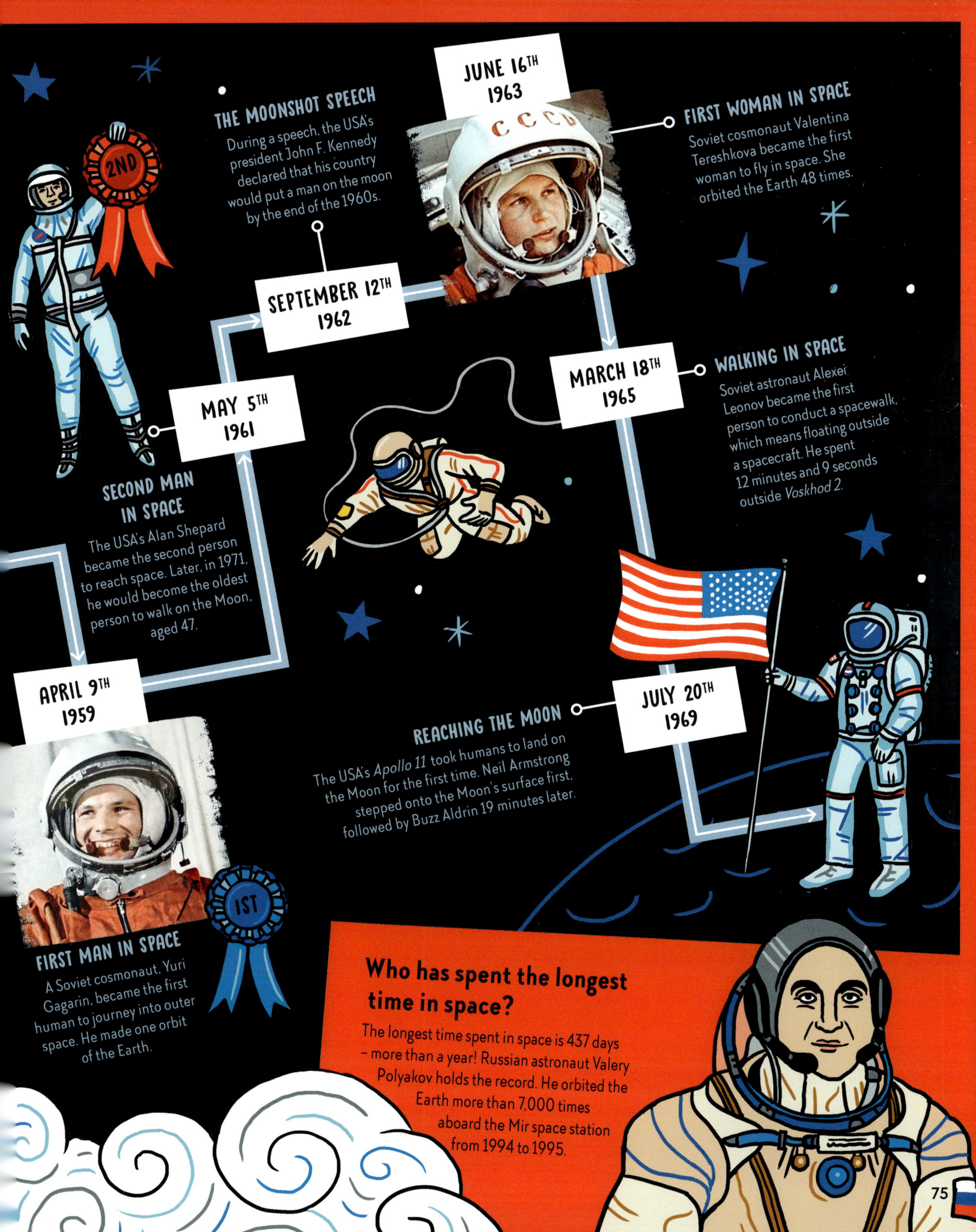

JUNE 16TH 1963

THE MOONSHOT SPEECH
During a speech, the USA's president John F. Kennedy declared that his country would put a man on the moon by the end of the 1960s.

FIRST WOMAN IN SPACE
Soviet cosmonaut Valentina Tereshkova became the first woman to fly in space. She orbited the Earth 48 times.

SEPTEMBER 12TH 1962

MARCH 18TH 1965

WALKING IN SPACE
Soviet astronaut Alexei Leonov became the first person to conduct a spacewalk, which means floating outside a spacecraft. He spent 12 minutes and 9 seconds outside *Voskhod 2*.

MAY 5TH 1961

SECOND MAN IN SPACE
The USA's Alan Shepard became the second person to reach space. Later, in 1971, he would become the oldest person to walk on the Moon, aged 47.

APRIL 9TH 1959

REACHING THE MOON
The USA's *Apollo 11* took humans to land on the Moon for the first time. Neil Armstrong stepped onto the Moon's surface first, followed by Buzz Aldrin 19 minutes later.

JULY 20TH 1969

FIRST MAN IN SPACE
A Soviet cosmonaut, Yuri Gagarin, became the first human to journey into outer space. He made one orbit of the Earth.

Who has spent the longest time in space?
The longest time spent in space is 437 days – more than a year! Russian astronaut Valery Polyakov holds the record. He orbited the Earth more than 7,000 times aboard the Mir space station from 1994 to 1995.

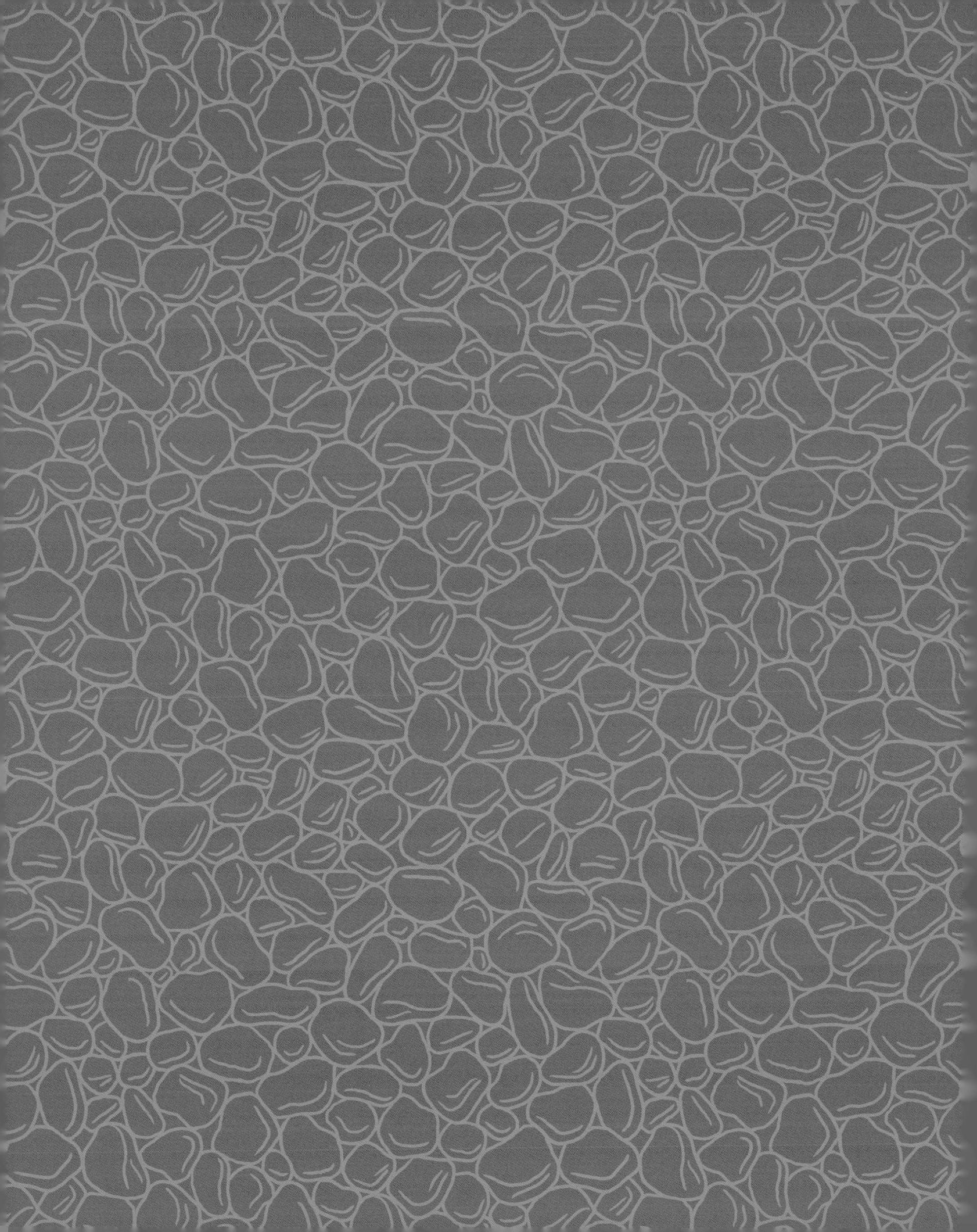

CHAPTER 6

BUILDING OUR WORLD

From around 11,000 years ago, humans went through three major changes. We began to stop living a nomadic, hunter-gatherer life, with the invention of farming. We built settlements and then cities. And, from around 3300 BCE, we discovered how to make the metal bronze. These changes helped us to build the world we live in today.

Cities became centres for education, science, and industry. People could share ideas with one another and work together to come up with more ideas. New inventions were needed to tackle problems faced by cities. Aqueducts were created to bring water to cities and the science of crop management became key to storing up enough food to feed everyone.

Metals and other materials were used to build bigger and better structures as time went on. Meanwhile, science helped us to overcome new problems.

MATERIALS

Thousands of years ago, humans relied on natural materials to create the items they needed, such as plants for clothing and rocks for weapons. Nowadays, science allows us to create new materials – known as synthetic materials – which can be used for all sorts of purposes.

WOOD

An age-old material, wood is one of the most popular natural materials still in use today. It can be hard and durable, like pine or oak, which are often used for making furniture, or soft, light, and easy to carve, like balsa wood, which is used in surfboards and boats. Wood is prized for its natural beauty.

Guitars are made from wood, but the type of wood used affects the sound it makes!

COAL

Coal has been humankind's main source of power since the Industrial Revolution. However, it is made up of 86% carbon and releases carbon dioxide into the atmosphere when it burns. Modern scientists are searching for more environmentally-friendly power resources to replace coal.

LITHIUM

The lightest metal, lithium, is known as "white gold", which shows just how valuable it is in the modern world. Lithium is a crucial component of rechargeable batteries, which power mobile phones, laptops, electric cars, and much more. These products are good for the environment, though lithium mining can have negative effects, such as pollution.

PAPER

Paper is an Egyptian invention, first made from a plant called papyrus. Chinese papermakers improved on it by adding other plant fibres. Paper is incredibly versatile – it can be as hard-wearing as paper money, or thin and soft as toilet paper. Plus, it can be recycled too!

PLASTICS

Plastic was invented in the early 1900s. Since then, many different types of plastic have been created, with all sorts of uses. Plastics are easily moulded into different shapes, can be made in different colours, and are sterile and clean for medical and food-packaging purposes. However, plastics do not degrade easily and are a huge source of waste and pollution.

NATURAL FIBRES

Fabrics made from natural fibres have been around for thousands of years or more. They were used for clothing, fishing nets, and rope. Linen is one of the oldest natural fabrics, made from the flax plant. Dyed flax fibres dating from 30,000 years ago have been found in the Dzudzuana Caves in Georgia.

GLASS

Glass is formed when sand melts at very high temperatures. Early Mesopotamian people created glass to make beads and jewellery in various colours. Nowadays, glass has many functional purposes too, such as windows, drinking glasses, and eye glasses – which all require the glass to be manufactured in specific ways.

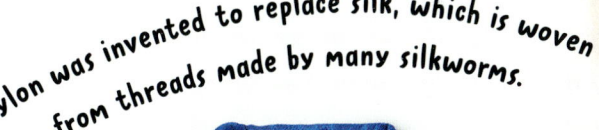

Nylon was invented to replace silk, which is woven from threads made by many silkworms.

LEATHER

Historically, leather was produced by tanning animal skins with acidic oak bark to stop them from decomposing. Leather is often used for clothing or items that require hard-wearing materials, such as satchels and belts. Many people, however, argue about the ethics of the leather industry and animal cruelty.

SYNTHETIC FIBRES

Science means we can create synthetic materials, which are often cheaper than natural ones. Synthetic fabrics can be engineered to have specific properties, such as strong, lightweight nylon, stain-resistant polyester, or Kevlar – a material that is five times stronger than steel and can be used for bulletproof vests.

Where did it begin?

The very first farmers may have lived in the Fertile Crescent – an area in West Asia around the Nile, Tigris, and Euphrates rivers. Crops would have grown well in the warm climate and there was plenty of water in the soil for them to drink.

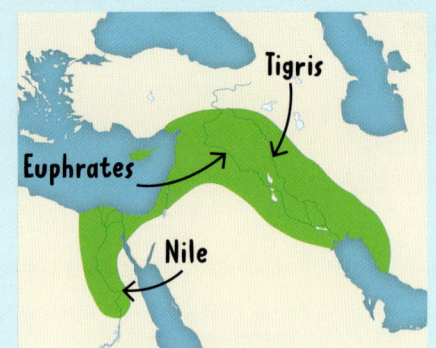

Tigris

Euphrates

Nile

The Fertile Crescent

FARMING

Learning to grow food helped communities to grow into cities.

People learned the seasons when seeds should be sown and when harvests would be ready.

Lentils

Wheat

Barley

Peas

Wheat was ground into flour to make bread.

We humans lived a wild existence as hunter gatherers for the first 100,000 years of our existence. If we could not find food growing, or if a herd of animals we were hunting moved, then we moved on to the next place. Then, suddenly, about 12,000 years ago, many humans stopped living as nomads and settled down to farm.

Agriculture, or farming, started at almost the same time in different parts of the world. The first farmers may have been helped by warmer weather brought on by climate change, which helped seedlings to grow. Barley was one of the first crops to be planted. It is quite easy to grow and can survive through bad weather. Another early crop that grew easily was a form of wheat, called einkorn. People also grew peas, chickpeas, and lentils. As farming began in more and more places, other species of crop were used. Potatoes, maize, and tomatoes were grown in South America, and rice was farmed in parts of Asia. The first animals to be raised and kept by farmers, at around the same time as the first crops, were goats, sheep, and cows.

Though people now had a steady supply of food, which could be stored and eaten during the winter when crops would not grow, they may not have been healthier than hunter gatherers. Our bodies need different nutrients and proteins to stay healthy. These can be found in different types of food, but early farmers tended to have only a few crops to eat. Hunter gatherers had a much more varied diet!

A place to call home

Hunter gatherers sheltered in caves or built shelters that could be easily taken apart, often from sticks and animal skins. With farming came the need for more permanent structures – the first stone and brick houses.

Ancient Egyptian plough

Farming tools

People invented tools to help them farm. The plough was a clawed tool pulled over land by animals. It churned the ground, so that soil lower down – which had not had its nutrients taken by past crops – was brought to the surface for new seeds.

Cows were kept for their meat and milk.

Houses in West Asia were built from clay bricks.

Over time people started to conduct scientific experiments to find out more about farming. We tried growing different types of plants, to see which gave us more food, or which was less likely to be eaten by bugs. We learned how to breed different strains of plant together – which meant growing plants with the best features of different parent plants. So, the size of our harvests grew.

As humans settled, our populations grew. Some settlements kept growing, until they became the first cities. You can find out what happened next on pages 82–83.

People developed a sweet tooth about 10,000 years ago, when sugar cane began to be farmed. Beekeeping began about 9,000 years ago, giving us honey.

People learned to cook food in different ways, such as in clay pots.

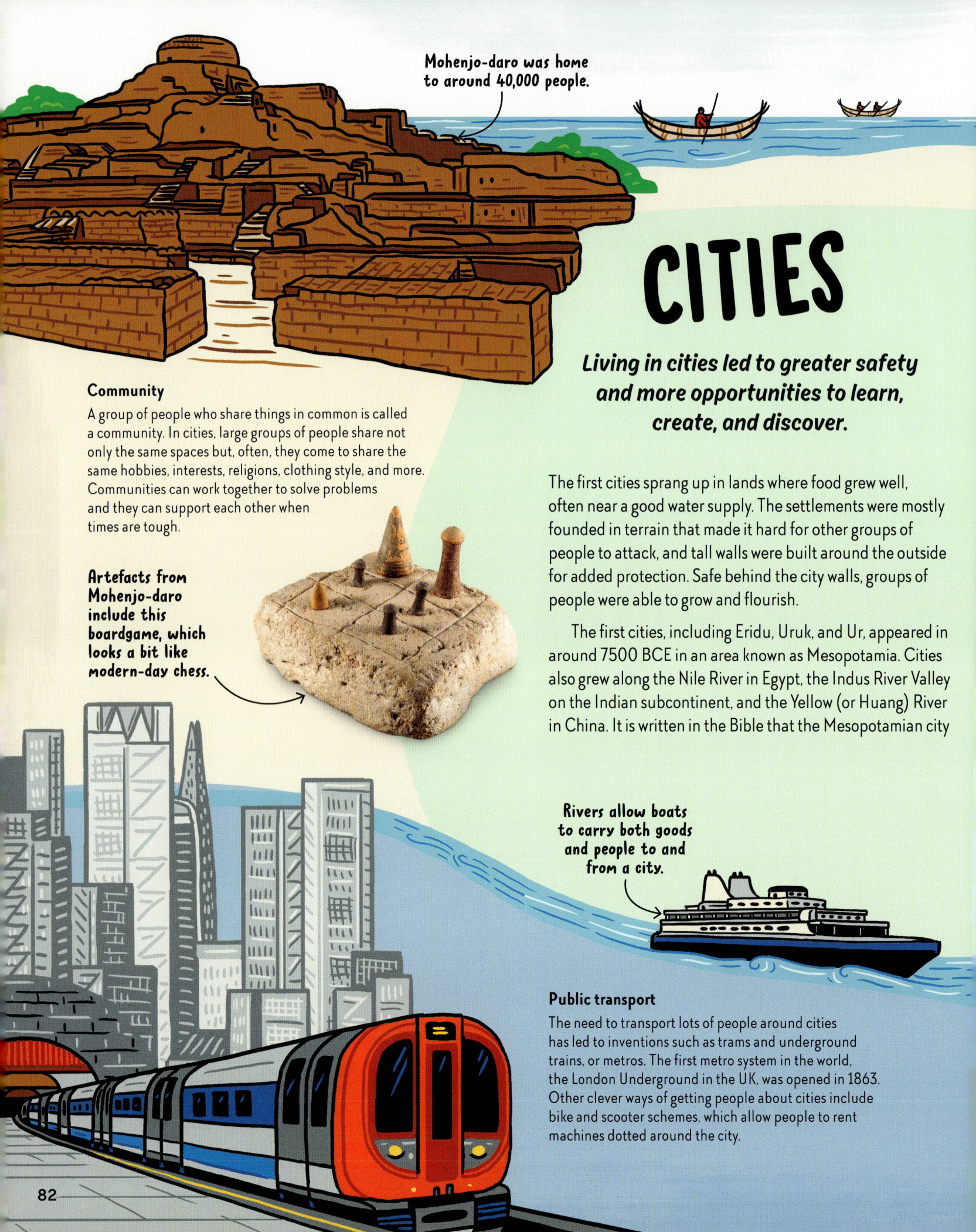

Mohenjo-daro was home to around 40,000 people.

CITIES

Living in cities led to greater safety and more opportunities to learn, create, and discover.

Community

A group of people who share things in common is called a community. In cities, large groups of people share not only the same spaces but, often, they come to share the same hobbies, interests, religions, clothing style, and more. Communities can work together to solve problems and they can support each other when times are tough.

Artefacts from Mohenjo-daro include this boardgame, which looks a bit like modern-day chess.

The first cities sprang up in lands where food grew well, often near a good water supply. The settlements were mostly founded in terrain that made it hard for other groups of people to attack, and tall walls were built around the outside for added protection. Safe behind the city walls, groups of people were able to grow and flourish.

The first cities, including Eridu, Uruk, and Ur, appeared in around 7500 BCE in an area known as Mesopotamia. Cities also grew along the Nile River in Egypt, the Indus River Valley on the Indian subcontinent, and the Yellow (or Huang) River in China. It is written in the Bible that the Mesopotamian city

Rivers allow boats to carry both goods and people to and from a city.

Public transport

The need to transport lots of people around cities has led to inventions such as trams and underground trains, or metros. The first metro system in the world, the London Underground in the UK, was opened in 1863. Other clever ways of getting people about cities include bike and scooter schemes, which allow people to rent machines dotted around the city.

Everything from grains to gemstones was sold in the Mesopotamian city of Babylon.

Markets

The marketplaces of early cities were busy hubs. People were able to make their riches selling goods here, instead of working as farmers or struggling to find customers for their products outside of the city. They could also discover different kinds of foods and pick up items they might treasure forever, such as jewellery or games.

of Nineveh was so huge that it took three days to cross – but this is probably an exaggeration!

City dwellers were able to work together doing lots of different jobs. They could also share knowledge and talk about their ideas. As a result, cities became centres for art, literature, education, philosophy, and science. As time went by, newer cities were often placed on trade routes so that journeys could be broken up into easy stages. This meant that ideas spread between cities, as well as between citizens.

Cities have their downsides, too. Rubbish and waste can build up. People are also packed more closely together. These factors can cause disease to spread more easily.

In ancient Rome's Curia Julia, a group of elders called the Senate met to discuss problems.

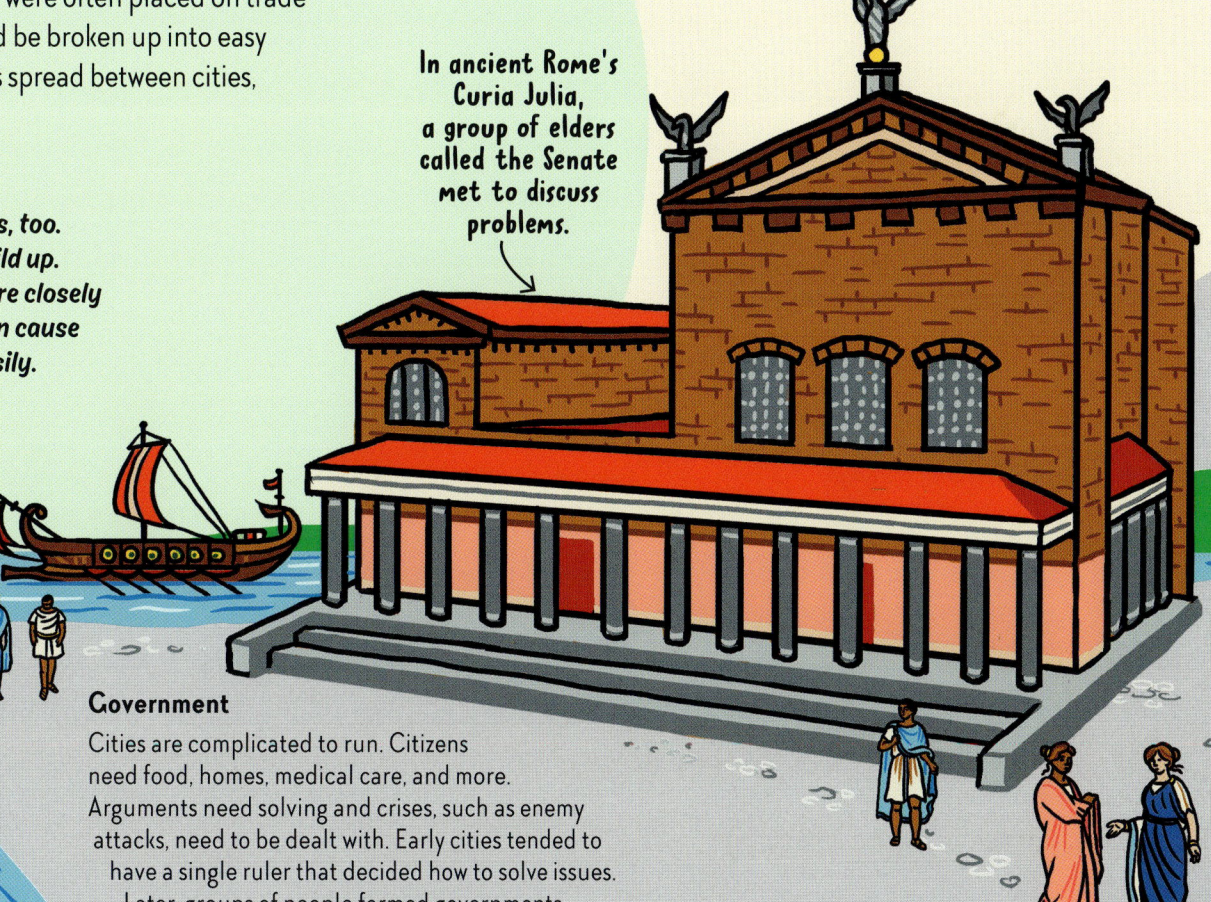

Government

Cities are complicated to run. Citizens need food, homes, medical care, and more. Arguments need solving and crises, such as enemy attacks, need to be dealt with. Early cities tended to have a single ruler that decided how to solve issues. Later, groups of people formed governments.

METALWORK

Working with metal has been going on since prehistory. Softer metals were carved by hand or with primitive tools to create jewellery. Over time, more and more processes have been developed that can shape, cut, or join metals together.

SMELTING

Metal-containing rocks (known as ores) are heated to very high temperatures to extract the molten (liquid) metal. This smelting process is how we get essential metals, including iron, copper, and silver – but the chemical reactions involved lead to a lot of pollution.

CASTING

Almost all metals are solids. To shape them, they are melted down and poured (or casted) into moulds. Casting is used to create all sorts of objects, including statues, jewellery, small machine parts, and tools. In fact, cast metal can be found in around 90 per cent of all manufactured goods.

HAMMERING

Hammering bends hot metal into shape. All decorative metalwork used to be done with a hammer. Some metals, such as gold, require just a little heat to make them soft enough to bend. Copper is harder, so it requires more. Hammering is still used today by blacksmiths to shape iron and steel, and craftspeople to create decorative objects.

GILDING

Covering objects with a thin layer of gold is cheaper than creating it out of pure gold. Wood, porcelain, paper, or other metals are often gilded to create jewellery or other grand objects, such as thrones and decorative picture frames. Gold that has been hammered into thin sheets is called gold leaf.

SOLDERING

Soldering joins two metals together without melting them. Instead, a third metal (or a metal alloy, which is a mixture of metals) is melted down and used to connect the original two together. As the solder cools, the join solidifies. Soldering has many uses, including electronic wiring, circuits, and plumbing.

The gold inlay stands out against the black metal on this 17th century Indian artefact.

INLAYING

A decorative technique, inlaying is when metal (usually a precious metal such as gold or silver) is set into the surface of another metal or material of a contrasting colour. Inlaying is an intricate process used to create special or ceremonial objects, including vases and furniture. It is also used to decorate musical instruments.

EMBOSSING

Metal embossing decorates a metal by raising part of its surface. This effect is achieved by placing a sheet of metal on its front, and then hammering a desired pattern into the underside. In this picture, a metalworker is using a hammer and stylus to emboss a piece of metal.

ENGRAVING

Engraving uses delicate tools to cut letters, shapes, or patterns into a piece of soft metal. It used to be done by hand, though nowadays there are specialised machines. Trophies or shields won by sports players are often engraved with their names and the date.

ENAMELLING

Enamelling is the process of using intense heat to fuse powdered glass to metal, resulting in a brilliantly coloured finish. It is used in the making of jewellery, objects of art, and for other decorative applications. This gold brooch uses enamelling for the vibrant colours of the flowers and leaves.

The first trade routes

One of the earliest shipping routes on record was between the Mesopotamian city of Uruk (now in Iraq) and a land called Meluhha, which was probably the Indus Valley civilization (now in Pakistan). Indus Valley stamp seals from around 2200 BCE have been found in Mesopotamia.

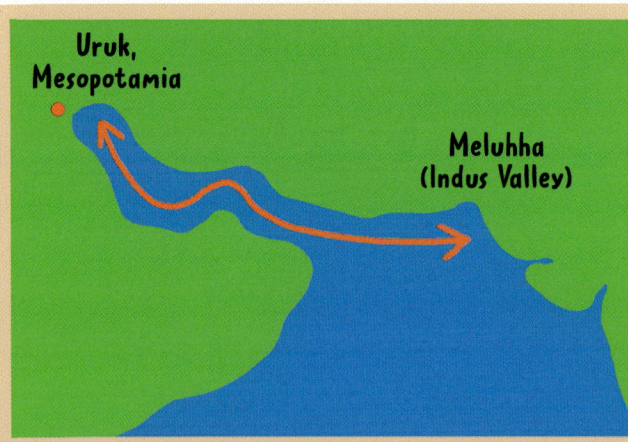

Uruk,
Mesopotamia

Meluhha
(Indus Valley)

Shells and beads from the Indus Valley have been unearthed at Mesopotamian archaeological sites.

SHIPPING

Discovering how to cross the sea enabled humans to travel, trade, and explore the Earth.

Most of the Earth is covered by oceans and seas. So, it was vitally important for humans to come up with a way to travel across water.

The first known boats were Mesopotamian river or coastal vessels from around 8,000 years ago. They were made of bundles of reeds coated with bitumen (tar). But it is almost certain that people ventured out to sea much earlier, based on the global spread of the human population.

Egyptian ships were more robust than their predecessors. Pottery from 4000 BCE depicts boats that probably traded along the Nile. The remains of 14 ships found at Abydos in Egypt show the design of wooden planks lashed together with

Spreading disease

While shipping furthers trade and spreads wealth across the continents, it can also spread something a little less pleasant: disease. In 1347, ships from Asia docked in the Mediterranean. On board were rats with fleas carrying the bubonic plague, which rapidly swept across Europe. Even today, our ability to travel between distant points of the globe increases the spread of germs.

The Transatlantic trade of enslaved people

Unfortunately, not all trade is good. In the 16th century, cargo ships were adapted to transport enslaved people across the Atlantic Ocean from Africa to North America, where they were sold and forced to do labour. While enslaving people was outlawed in the 19th century, some criminals still smuggle humans across the seas today.

Enslaved people in the Americas grew crops, which were sent to Europe. There, they were made into rum and other products, which were sent to Africa to be exchanged for more enslaved people.

woven straps. These ships were more than 23 m (75 ft) long – and likely sailed beyond the Nile, into the Mediterranean.

Over time, shipping evolved to meet the needs of developing civilizations. The vessels required more space for cargo and crew, and as ships grew in size, increased power and stability was needed too. Engineers designed sails in different shapes using various construction techniques, aiming to harness the wind while keeping the ships on course.

Seagoing is hazardous, and continued innovation has improved the speed and safety of ships – from adding masts, sails, rudders, and keels, to installing weapons, engines, and navigation systems. The ships of today are vastly more seaworthy than those of 8,000 years ago, though the sea remains a powerful and unpredictable force.

The first circumnavigation of the globe was achieved by Portuguese explorer Ferdinand Magellan. It took more than two years, and Magellan was killed in battle on the way home.

The Suez Canal allows ships to cut across Egypt, but they can get stuck and cause huge shipping delays!

Modern shipping

Today, ships can transport huge amounts of cargo – and they do it by stacking large containers. The biggest container ships are around 400 m (1,312 ft) long and can carry 24,000 containers. Deep, wide canals have been dug in some places, to allow ships to cut through countries rather than sail all the way around.

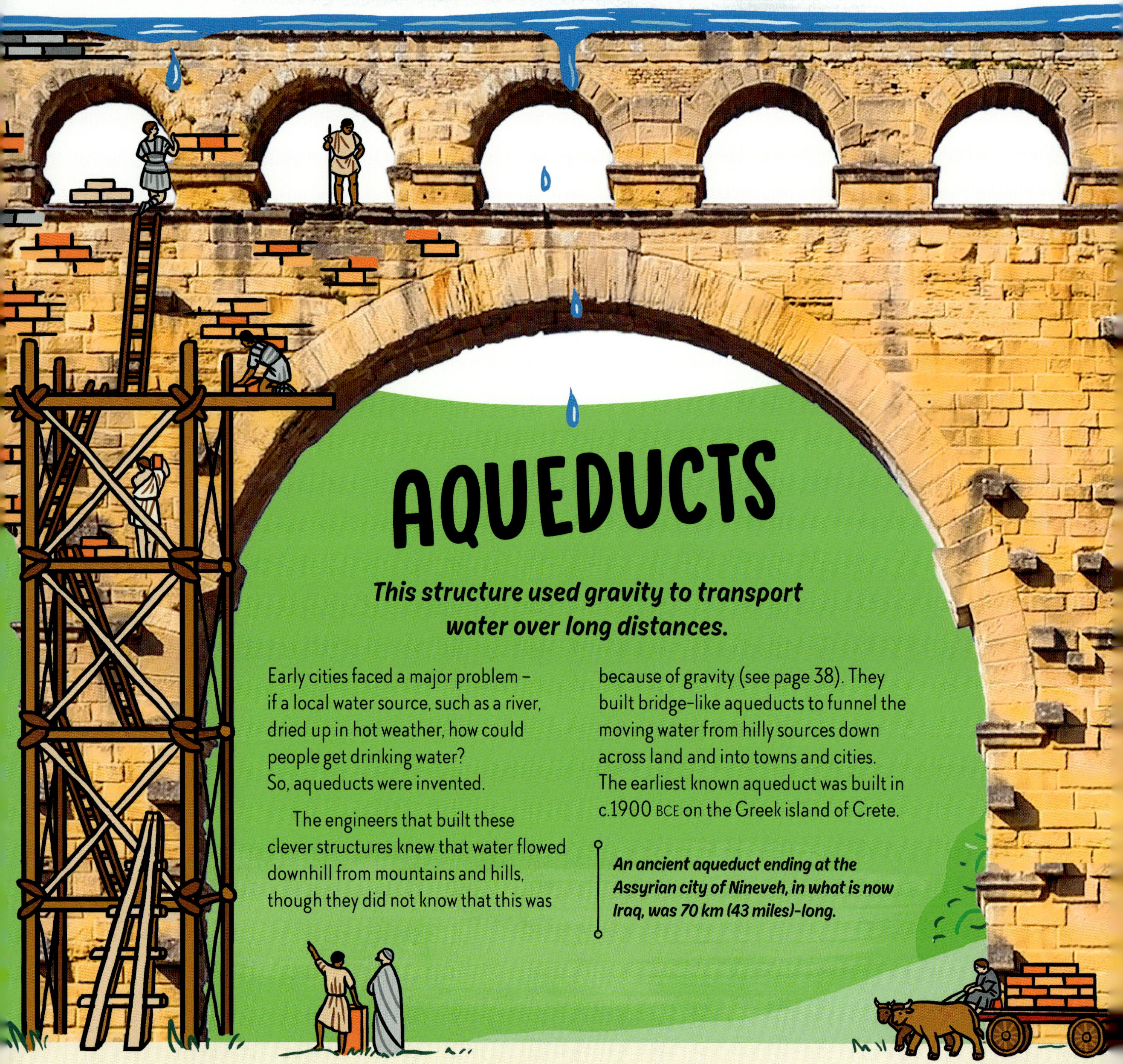

AQUEDUCTS

This structure used gravity to transport water over long distances.

Early cities faced a major problem – if a local water source, such as a river, dried up in hot weather, how could people get drinking water? So, aqueducts were invented.

The engineers that built these clever structures knew that water flowed downhill from mountains and hills, though they did not know that this was because of gravity (see page 38). They built bridge-like aqueducts to funnel the moving water from hilly sources down across land and into towns and cities. The earliest known aqueduct was built in c.1900 BCE on the Greek island of Crete.

An ancient aqueduct ending at the Assyrian city of Nineveh, in what is now Iraq, was 70 km (43 miles)-long.

How were they made?

The ancient Romans built some of the most impressive aqueducts – a number of which are still standing today. Roman aqueducts had stone channels to carry the water, raised up on arches made from concrete and waterproof cement. Clay or lead tubes, called siphons, were built to carry water upwards from reservoirs. The Romans also invented stopcocks, which blocked off the flow of the water if it rushed too powerfully. Many more improvements were made over time – too many to fit here, in fact!

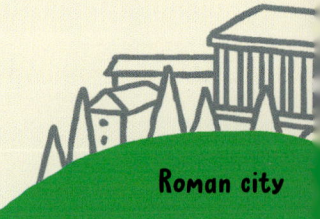

Roman city

What came next?

Modern aqueducts

You might not see arched aqueducts stretching overland today. But, hidden away beneath the ground, modern aqueducts carry much more water for far greater distances than their ancient counterparts. New York City, USA, home to about 8.5 million people, gets its water from three main aqueduct systems. These structures carry 6.8 billion litres (1.8 billion gallons) of water a day from up to 190 km (120 miles) away.

Water treatment plants

Over time, people worked out how to clean used water. This meant that cities needed less fresh water from further away. Modern pipes often carry dirty water to nearby water treatment plants, where it is cleaned and sent back. Find out how water is cleaned on page 132.

Builders stood on scaffolding made from wood.

Arched section over valley

Siphon carrying water

Reservoir

GUNPOWDER

The science of explosions led to deadly inventions.

How do cannons work?

Gunpowder is added to a compartment at the back of a cannon, with the cannonball in front of it. When the gunpowder is set alight it burns extremely fast, which causes gases to expand very quickly. The pressure, or pushing force, from the gases launches the cannonball from the mouth of the cannon.

More gunpowder is added each time the cannon is reloaded.

In around the 9th century, Chinese alchemists raced to create a potion that would allow their emperor to live forever. Instead, they created an explosive mixture called gunpowder.

The mixture was soon used to make weapons in Asia. Bombs made from gunpowder could destroy anything near them and were tossed over enemy city walls using catapults. A gunpowder explosion could be used to propel (push out) cannonballs from cannons at great speed. Soon, smaller, hand-held weapons were using gunpowder to launch projectiles in a similar way.

Gunpowder weapons made wars far more deadly than before. But over time, the mixture began to be used for nonviolent purposes, too. Explosions cleared land for building waterways, railways, and roads, and useful rocks and minerals could be blown out of the ground in mines.

The more gunpowder used, the bigger the explosion.

What came next?

Firearms

The first handheld weapon that used gunpowder was invented in the 900s. It was called the fire lance and it fired arrows. Hand-held cannons followed in the 1200s. But these weapons needed two hands to operate – one to hold a match to the gunpowder and one to aim the gun. From the 1400s, guns that could be shot with one hand were made. When fired, the gun touched a slow-burning match to the gunpowder.

Gunpowder that has been kept dry is unlikely to explode unexpectedly.

Fireworks

The first fireworks were created from sticks of bamboo filled with gunpowder – which exploded with a bang but did not have the bright colours we see in fireworks today. It wasn't until the 1830s that Italian inventors added metals such as barium to fireworks to create colours.

DYNAMITE

This invention made mining easier and war more deadly.

Up until the mid-1800s, explosives were often unstable. This meant that they could blow up unexpectedly and injure nearby people. Alfred Nobel (1833–1896), the son of an explosive maker, wanted to invent a safer explosive.

One of the main uses for explosives during Alfred's time was in mines, where rocks and minerals were taken from the ground. Explosives could blow the rocks from the ground much more quickly than a miner could chip them out with handheld tools. But, as well as being unstable, the available explosives weren't always strong enough to do their job. So, in 1867, Alfred created dynamite – a safer and more powerful type of explosive.

Dynamite contains an explosive called nitroglycerin. It had been used in explosives

before, but it was very unstable. Alfred mixed the nitroglycerin with the powder of a special type of white rock, called diatomite. This made it much less likely to go off accidentally. The mixture was then rolled into a stick and a blasting cap was added to the end. When lit, the cap went off with a small explosion, which set off the dynamite's much bigger explosion. Finally, a long fuse connected to the blasting cap gave people time to get away from the explosion after lighting the fuse.

Dynamite made mining much easier and safer, but it was also used during wars to harm enemy soldiers. Alfred later created a prize for people who had done good things for the world, to try to make up for the harm caused by his invention.

Sticks of dynamite could be bound together to make bigger explosions.

DYNAMITE

Fuse

What next?

A safer way to build

Dynamite is 1,000 times more powerful than gunpowder, which was the most popular explosive before. It made construction projects much quicker, and could be used to carve out ditches or to create tunnels through hills for trainlines and canals. Soon, countries were connected like never before.

A world of weapons

Dynamite also became a weapon. It was used by armies at war and by individuals who wanted to do harm to those around them. However, by World War One (1914–1918), newer types of explosives were being used.

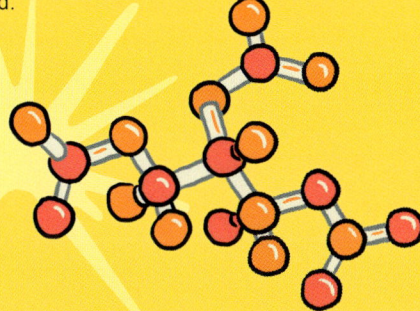

A peaceful prize

Alfred made a lot of money from dynamite and his other inventions. He left much of it to be used as Nobel Prize money, to reward people who do good work for humanity.

Most fuses took around two minutes to burn down to the sticks of dynamite.

Alfred Nobel created 355 inventions in his lifetime, including gas meters and artificial rubber.

NOBEL PRIZE MEDAL

The Nobel Prize

Categories

There are prizes for six different subjects: Physics, Chemistry, Physiology or Medicine, Literature, Economics, and Peace.

Nominees

The Nobel Committee asks 3,000 people who they think should win a prize that year. After hearing their suggestions, 300 nominees (potential winners) are selected.

Voting

The prize's committee passes the names of their chosen nominees on to a different, expert group for each prize. These groups then vote for their winner.

Ceremony

The awards ceremony takes place in Alfred Nobel's birthplace of Stockholm, Sweden. Each winner gives a lecture to inform people about their work, and everyone celebrates at a grand banquet.

Prizes

Nobel Prize medals are given to the winners, as well as money and a qualification called a diploma. The medals have different designs depending on the category.

NOBEL PRIZE WINNERS

Many Nobel Prize winners have changed the world for the better. But it's important to remember that they did not work alone – virtually all science is a group effort. A small number of prizes were also awarded to people whose work went on to do great harm.

LORD RAYLEIGH

Mathematician and scientist John William Strutt (known as Lord Rayleigh) won the Nobel Prize for his research on how light scatters, which officially answers the question, "Why is the sky blue?"

PHYSICS - 1903   **CHEMISTRY - 1911**

MARIE CURIE

Marie Curie was ground-breaking in many ways. Women in Poland were not allowed to attend university, but that didn't stop her. She moved to Paris and studied physics and maths. In 1903, she was the first woman to win a Nobel Prize – which she shared with her husband Pierre and fellow physicist Henri Becquerel for their work on radiation. In 1911, Curie won a second Nobel Prize, this time in Chemistry for her work on radioactivity. This made her the first person to ever win two Nobel Prizes (a record that was only matched in 1962), and she remains one of only two people to have won two Nobel Prizes in different fields.

Since the Nobel Prize Ceremony began in 1901, more than 900 people have won, but only five people have won twice!

NIELS BOHR

Danish physicist Niels Bohr won the Nobel Prize for his research on the structure of atoms. His ideas about how electrons orbit around a neutron are still the basis of how we understand atoms today.

BARBARA McCLINTOCK

Barbara McClintock researched maize (corn) chromosomes for her entire career. Her studies led to new discoveries about how genes work and how they are positioned within chromosomes. Her Nobel Prize in 1983 was for research she'd published 20 years earlier. Unfortunately, it was (and remains) difficult for women to get the same recognition as men.

PHYSICS - 1922   **MEDICINE - 1983**

IVAN PAVLOV

Pavlov left the Church to study maths and physiology at St Petersburg University. His work on nerve function of the heart, stomach, and pancreas in dogs transformed physiology. I read his book *Conditioned Reflexes* when I was thirteen; it totally changed my thinking about science.

FRITZ HABER

Haber's story is of "wicked chemistry which saved the world's population". He won the Nobel Prize for Chemistry for developing ways of making ammonia (synthesis). This is vital for fertilisers and improving one third of the world's food supply. However, this work also led to poison gas in the First World War, and his Zyklon B was used to exterminate more than a million people.

CHEMISTRY - 1964

DOROTHY HODGKIN

Fascinated by crystals, Hodgkin was one of two girls allowed to study chemistry at her grammar school. She later taught at Oxford. Her use of X-ray crystallography led to the mapping of penicillin and insulin molecules, making it possible to manufacture these life-saving medicines.

MAY-BRITT MOSER

Norwegian neuroscientist May-Britt Moser won a Nobel Prize for her understanding of brain cells – how they help us perceive our body's position, and how they help us think in general.

MEDICINE - 1949

ANTÓNIO EGAS MONIZ

If there was a Nobel Prize for the wrong achievement, Moniz would be a perfect candidate. The Portuguese doctor is famous for work on lobotomy for severe mental depression, but twenty years earlier, he developed radiology of the brain's blood supply, called "angiography" to improve surgical treatments. Lobotomy later had many disastrous consequences, but he should have won his prize for identifying brain tumours.

GM CROPS

Blight-stricken potato

Blight-resistant potato

NON-GM TOMATO

Learning to modify crops was a step towards solving the problem of hunger.

Around two billion people on Earth need more food. It is crucial not to waste food or the resources needed to grow crops, such as water – but genetic science can help solve the problem of starvation, too. Genetically modified (GM) crops can yield more food, grow faster, and be resistant to drought and infection.

Humans have been trying to improve crops for 10,000 years. Interbreeding strains of wheat, which meant picking two different parent plants with good qualities, often made the grains of new plants larger or tastier. Nowadays, we can modify plants by changing their DNA (see pages 50–51). X-rays can cause random DNA changes (mutations) in plants, and we can then choose to breed those with desired characteristics. We can make more targeted changes using bacteria or viruses to transfer new DNA into a plant's cells. Gene editing is more efficient still, allowing a short, specific DNA fragment to be inserted at a precise position in the plant's genome.

Sometimes DNA changes can have unexpected results. It may be harmful to the plant or, occasionally, to humans. Much testing is now done and most countries control, regulate, and label GM foods. Modified crops can make lots of money, too, which can be used to fund research and further technological improvements. Thanks to these techniques, we now make plants that can help the hungry: disease-resistant potatoes, tomatoes that stay fresh for longer, sweeter pineapples, and healthier rice.

What came before?

Mendel's pea plants

In the 1850s and '60s, biologist Gregor Mendel interbred pea plants with varying characteristics, such as height and flower colour. His findings helped us understand how inherited genes are passed on. He also defined the idea of dominant and recessive genes (genes that are more or less likely to be passed on).

Golden rice

GM TOMATO

Normal rice

Normal pineapple

Pink pineapple

How was it made?

To genetically modify a plant, scientists alter the plant's DNA, which instructs the plant to grow in a certain way. Bacteria and viruses are commonly used in GM processes because they are able to transfer their own DNA into the cells of their host.

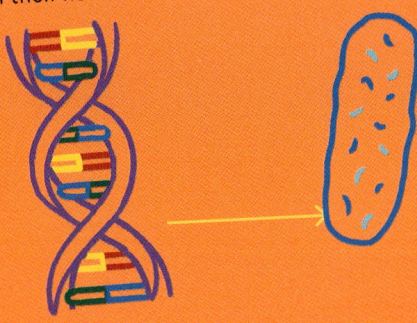

Bacteria

Scientists identify the gene or DNA sequence they want to introduce to a plant, for example, the gene that will delay tomato skin from softening. They transfer this gene to bacteria.

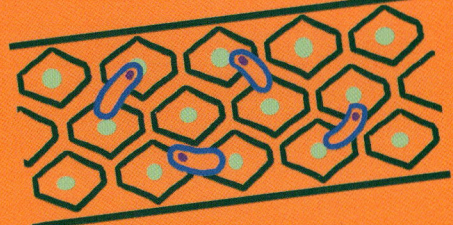

Plant tissue

The bacteria are introduced to the plant, and they insert their DNA into the plant's cells. The plant's genome now contains the new DNA sequence. It has been genetically modified.

Modified plant

The modified plant tissue is used to grow a new plant, which will have the desired characteristics – in this case, tomatoes that don't soften as quickly as regular tomatoes.

CHAPTER 7

EVERYDAY SCIENCE

Scientific tools, discoveries, and inventions can be seen all around you. A campfire can produce vivid colours depending on the chemical contents of its fuel. It might be tinged yellow with sodium or greenish–blue if there is copper in the soil below. Mathematics may have begun with early humans counting the members of their group to make sure no one was missing and is now used to count the entire population of the Earth. Maths equations help us to understand incredible ideas about the nature of curved space–time, or the position of electrons in orbit around an atomic nucleus. Measurements are central to science – they allow us to describe the smallest particles and the vast size of the universe.

Everyday inventions use scientific theories, too. Soap can kill bacteria, refrigerators work through the cooling and heating of coolants, and electricity was first generated in an experiment.

How were fires built?

The ingredients of fire are heat, fuel, and a gas called oxygen. Oxygen is found in the air, so early humans simply needed to work out how to create heat and what they could use as fuel. Our ancestors probably made heat by hitting certain rocks together. The fuel would likely have been dry twigs or other parts of plants.

Striking rocks together can create hot sparks.

Burnt fishbones and barley were found left over from a meal cooked in Israel 780,000 years ago.

FIRE

Flames helped our ancestors to survive and thrive.

Imagine how puzzling, mysterious, beautiful, and terrifying wild fire must have seemed to our early ancestors. Eventually we were able to capture and use it, but this took over a million years of activity.

It is not known just when humans first created fires, but burnt and scorched materials can be clues to help us work out the dates. This type of evidence has been found from nearly two million years ago. Modern humans did not exist then, but the firemakers were close relatives of our species.

Our ancestors slowly learned how to use fire in different ways. It could keep them warm at night and during cold weather. Fire scared away predators, such as cave lions. It allowed humans to see at night, which gave them more time to finish tasks. Archaeologists think that our ancestors began cooking with fire around 1.8 million years ago, and that fire was used to make stronger tools from around 300,000 years ago. Humans even used fire to change the landscapes around them, by burning trees to clear land.

A fire's warmth and light, and the safety it provided from wild beasts, was essential for human survival.

What came next?

Cooking

The human body is not able to get as much protein and fat from raw meat as it is from cooked meat. Scientists think that the extra protein and fat from cooked meat helped the smaller brain of our early ancestors to develop into the larger brain that we have today.

Toolmaking

Fire can change materials. A rock called flint can be made stronger if it is burnt. Flakes of flint blades burnt 300,000 years ago have been found in Morocco. From around 7000 BCE, people learned that certain rocks could be heated to release metals for making into tools and weapons.

Land clearing

In the past, many parts of the world were covered in thick forest. Early humans learned to use fire to burn down trees to clear land to live on. From around 10,000 years ago, people began to use cleared land to raise animals for meat and milk, and to grow grains and vegetables to eat.

MATHS

Mathematics allows us to count our possessions. This enables us to assign a value to things and trade with others. The modern world is built on trade, finance, and commerce, which all rely on maths. Over the centuries, many different cultures and civilizations made major contributions to our understanding of numbers.

ARITHMETIC

Arithmetic is the study of numbers and how they interact with each other. It includes the basic calculations, including addition, subtraction, multiplication, and division. The ancient Greeks had nine symbols for the nine numbers but no zero. Zero came later.

MESOPOTAMIAN NUMERALS

Five thousand years ago, the Mesopotamians had a sound knowledge of maths, including square roots, fractions, and equations. They created the first number system, which was made up of 60 base units. We still use sets of 60 to measure time (seconds and minutes) and angles (360° in a circle).

GEOMETRY

From the Greek words for "land" and "measure", geometry was invented as a method to understand and describe the world around us. It deals with space, shapes, area, volume, distance, angles, and proportions. An Egyptian papyrus from 1150 BCE is one of the earliest texts to contain geometry.

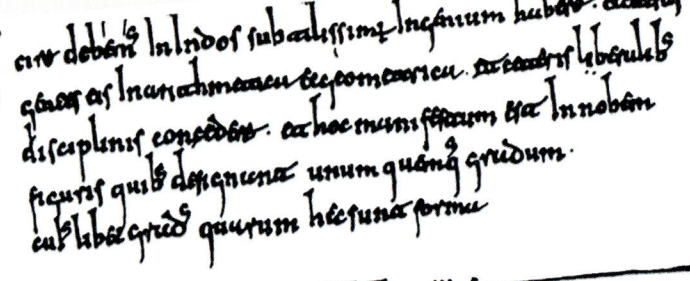

ARABIC NUMERALS

Arabic numerals are those used all over the world: 1, 2, 3, 4, 5, 6, 7, 8, 9, and 0. First devised in India in the 6th–7th centuries, they were spread to Europe by Arab mathematicians and were adopted for their logic and simplicity.

CALCULUS

Calculus measures curves, movement, and velocity. In the 18th century, mathematicians Gottfried Leibniz and Isaac Newton quarrelled about who thought of calculus first. It seems they both contributed to this mathematical advance simultaneously.

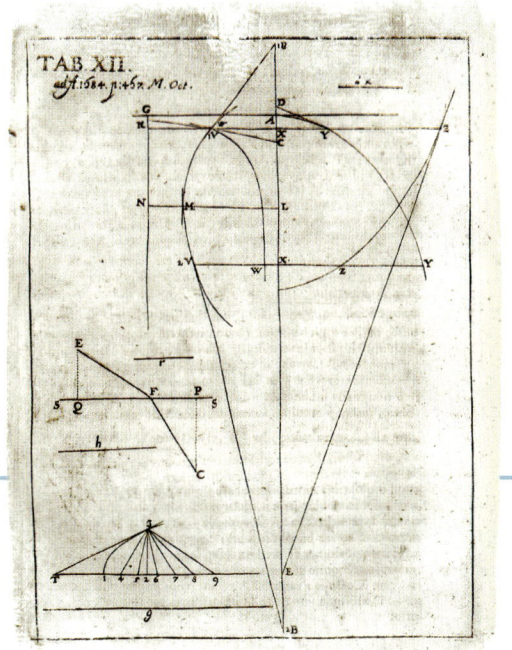

ALGEBRA

Algebra is the study of equations. By replacing numbers in an equation with Roman letters (such as x), algebra enables us to work out a formula for solving the equation with various different numbers. Algebra can be applied to all aspects of life – from calculating financial formulas and analysing sports strategy, to launching a rocket and even working out how hard to throw your rubbish so it will land in the bin!

Persian mathematician Muhammad ibn Musa al-Khwarizmi first used the word al-jabr to describe this area of maths.

COMPUTER CODE

Computer programs are built on mathematics. To tell a computer what to do, we need to write a series of instructions (also called code). But computers don't understand our spoken language. Coding languages follow specific rules and formulas, which are converted into binary (a string of 1s and 0s) inside the computer's machinery.

DECIMALS

Maths doesn't just deal with whole numbers (known as integers), it needs to account for parts of a number. This might sound obvious, but until the invention of decimals, there wasn't a precise way to express partial numbers. Decimals break down integers in tens, so 0.1 represents one-tenth of the integer 1, while 0.01 represents one-hundredth of 1. (Fractions also express partial numbers, but they were invented later.)

MEASUREMENTS

Science would be impossible if we could not measure.

Before measurements existed, people had to guess how much material they would need to build a home, or the amount of ingredients they would need to cook a dish or to mix medicine. Measurements allowed us to pass on exact instructions for the best things we had made, and to create even better versions.

One of the earliest known measurements is the cubit, which was used in ancient Egypt from around 3000 BCE. Like many early measurements, the cubit was based on a body part – it was the length of a man's forearm. As time went on, and more things were designed, built, and invented, exact measurements were needed.

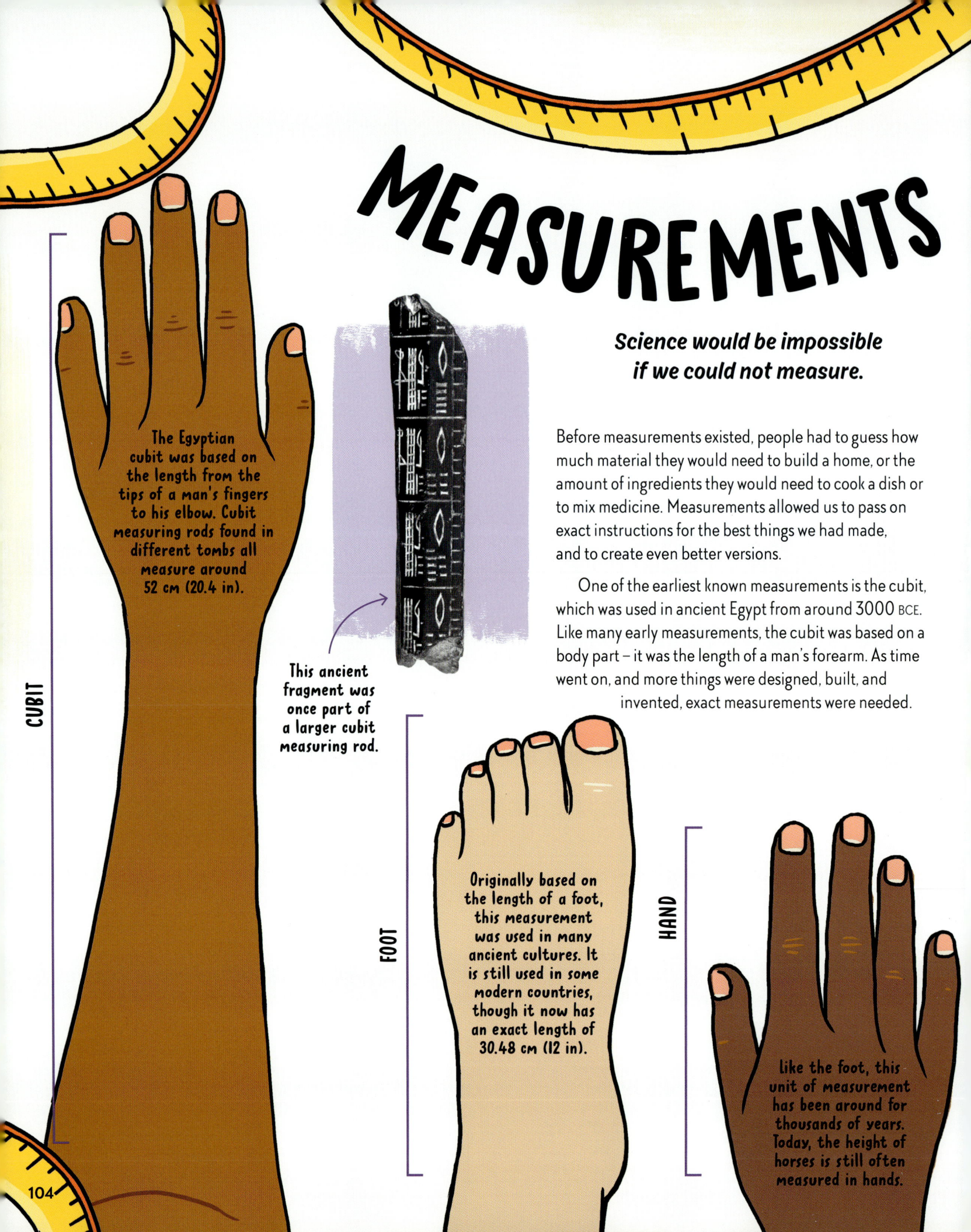

CUBIT

The Egyptian cubit was based on the length from the tips of a man's fingers to his elbow. Cubit measuring rods found in different tombs all measure around 52 cm (20.4 in).

This ancient fragment was once part of a larger cubit measuring rod.

FOOT

Originally based on the length of a foot, this measurement was used in many ancient cultures. It is still used in some modern countries, though it now has an exact length of 30.48 cm (12 in).

HAND

Like the foot, this unit of measurement has been around for thousands of years. Today, the height of horses is still often measured in hands.

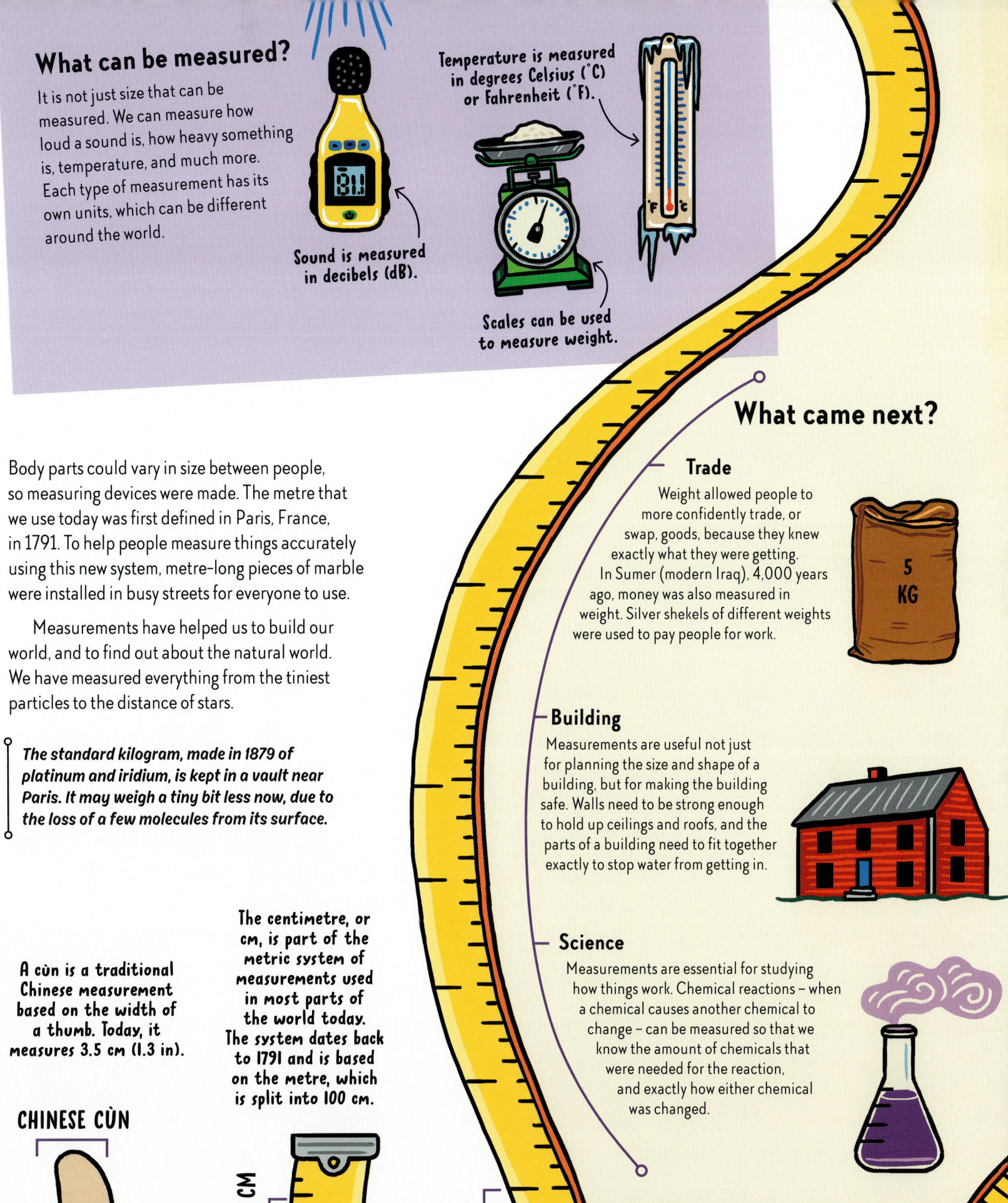

What can be measured?

It is not just size that can be measured. We can measure how loud a sound is, how heavy something is, temperature, and much more. Each type of measurement has its own units, which can be different around the world.

Sound is measured in decibels (dB).

Temperature is measured in degrees Celsius (°C) or Fahrenheit (°F).

Scales can be used to measure weight.

Body parts could vary in size between people, so measuring devices were made. The metre that we use today was first defined in Paris, France, in 1791. To help people measure things accurately using this new system, metre-long pieces of marble were installed in busy streets for everyone to use.

Measurements have helped us to build our world, and to find out about the natural world. We have measured everything from the tiniest particles to the distance of stars.

The standard kilogram, made in 1879 of platinum and iridium, is kept in a vault near Paris. It may weigh a tiny bit less now, due to the loss of a few molecules from its surface.

A cùn is a traditional Chinese measurement based on the width of a thumb. Today, it measures 3.5 cm (1.3 in).

CHINESE CÙN

The centimetre, or cm, is part of the metric system of measurements used in most parts of the world today. The system dates back to 1791 and is based on the metre, which is split into 100 cm.

METRIC CM

INCH

What came next?

Trade

Weight allowed people to more confidently trade, or swap, goods, because they knew exactly what they were getting. In Sumer (modern Iraq), 4,000 years ago, money was also measured in weight. Silver shekels of different weights were used to pay people for work.

Building

Measurements are useful not just for planning the size and shape of a building, but for making the building safe. Walls need to be strong enough to hold up ceilings and roofs, and the parts of a building need to fit together exactly to stop water from getting in.

Science

Measurements are essential for studying how things work. Chemical reactions – when a chemical causes another chemical to change – can be measured so that we know the amount of chemicals that were needed for the reaction, and exactly how either chemical was changed.

Inches are part of the UK's imperial system and the US's system of customary units.

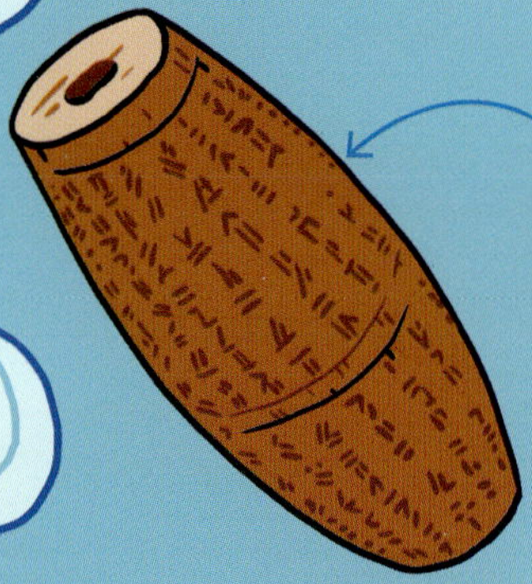

Some containers from ancient Babylon have "fats boiled with ashes" written on the outside. This fat and ash mixture was an early type of soap.

SOAP OR DYE?

Though the word "soap" comes from the Latin word, "sapo", the Romans did not actually use soap. Their history books mention soap as something that was used in Gaul, a region in western Europe, to dye women's hair red. The dye's main ingredient was fat.

What came next?

Public baths

Both the ancient Greeks and Romans built public baths, which became hubs where people could chat and share news. They used oil to clean themselves in place of soap. The oil was applied and scraped off, taking grime with it.

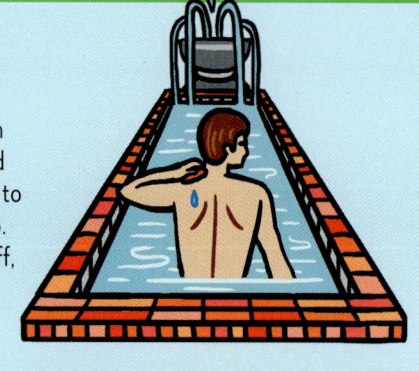

Detergents

Today, we usually wash clothes with detergents. These were introduced during the First World War because fats for making soaps were scarce. Synthetic (human-made) fats, made with a base of fuel oil, were used to make these new types of soap.

SOAP

This concoction helped us to stay clean and healthy – long before we knew what germs were.

Your skin is constantly coming into contact with the outside world. Your fingers often touch things – you are touching this book right now! And that means you might be picking up germs from surfaces. Lots of these germs are harmless, but some might cause you to get ill. Up until the 1800s people did not know that germs existed. But they used soap to wash away grime from their skin and clothes –and this unknowingly washed away germs, too.

The first records of soap come from the Middle East, where writing was invented. But soap may have been made earlier than we think, by people who did not write.

The earliest human-made soaps are thought to have been made in Babylon, in what is now Iraq, in 2800 BCE. We even know how the soap might have been made – in the reign of Nabonidus, the last King of Babylon, a recipe for soap consisted of uhulu [ashes], cypress oil, and sesame seeds. Over time, animal fats began to be used as a main ingredient for some soaps, instead of oil.

Chemical reactions were at the heart of early soap making. In Sumer, in what is now Iraq, in 2500 BCE, soap was produced by heating a mixture of oil and wood ash. Mixing substances in their workshops, these soap makers were some of the first scientists.

How was it made?

Most early soaps combined a fat or oil with other substances. Both ancient Egyptian and ancient Babylonian soaps added substances that would help release oil from dirty skin, such as tree ash.

Mixing ingredients
Tree ash, cypress oil, and sesame seeds were mixed in a pot and heated.

Solid soap
A liquid soap mixture could be poured into a mould and left to harden into a block.

Hand sanitizer
These cleaning products kill germs. The sanitizers evaporate, or turn into vapour, quickly. This leaves skin dry so there's no need to use a towel, which might carry germs. Sanitizers have been used in hospitals for 40 years, and were especially useful during the Covid pandemic.

ELECTRICAL ENERGY

The kite had a metal wire attached to the top.

This powerful force was once only seen in nature.

The metal key conducted electricity.

The great Greek natural scientist Pliny the Elder described how tree resin (amber) could attract dry leaves in about 77 CE. Much later, in 1600, the term "electricity" (well, "electricus") was first used to describe amber's ability to attract, by English scientist William Gilbert. This was a step forward in the understanding of electricity, but there was much still to be learned.

In the 1700s, Benjamin Franklin, a US politician, scientist, writer, and philosopher (in short, a bit of a clever clogs) dedicated much of his time to understanding electricity. He recognised that it flows along a wire between electrodes. He was also one of the first to prove that lightning was electricity, by flying a kite in a storm in 1752, with a key attached to the string. Not such a clever clogs after all, but luckily his kite was not struck by lightning and he picked up a smaller electrical charge from the storm with a spark from the key. Other scientists tried the experiment and were electrocuted – definitely not something you should try at home!

Experiments with electricity continued apace, and in 1819 it was discovered that electricity and magnetism (see page 68) are linked. Finally, in 1831, English scientist Michael Faraday worked out that moving a magnet around a copper coil can make, or generate, electricity. He had invented the electric generator.

This generator spun a copper coil between the arms of a U-shaped magnet.

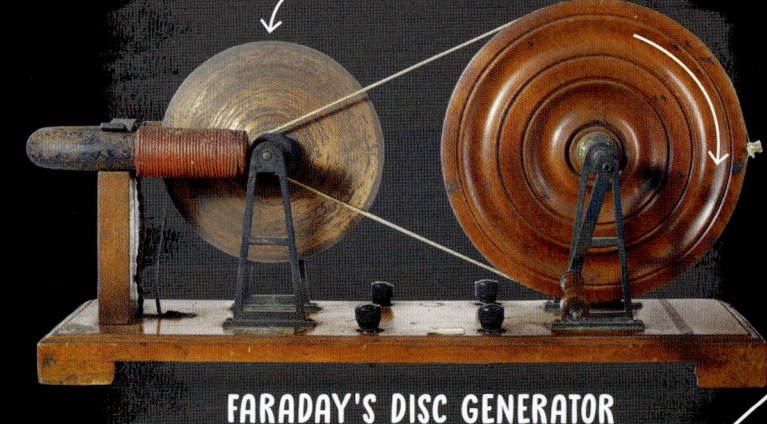

FARADAY'S DISC GENERATOR

What came next?

Grid power

Large amounts of electricity generation came after Faraday's invention. Wires to carry this electricity into homes and businesses were added to cities, creating the electrified world we live in. But we still have not found efficient batteries to store electricity on the grid, which is one of our greatest needs.

Communication

Without electricity, we would not be able to communicate as we do today – instantly and from wherever we are – with handheld electrical machines. The first of these communication inventions was the telegraph (see page 120), which was followed by the telephone.

Getting around

Electric vehicles do not produce fumes that pollute the air. But we still need to find ways to produce enough electricity to power them without burning fossil fuels in power stations and releasing pollution. Researchers now study ways to capture the fumes from power stations and get rid of them.

The string had a dry piece of silk at the end, which Franklin thought would stop him being electrocuted.

Lightning rods

Benjamin Franklin's kite experiment showed that lightning is electricity, and that it will travel down metal wire. He realised that a tall metal rod could also conduct electricity, and that this could be used to channel lightning safely to the ground so that it would not hit buildings and damage them.

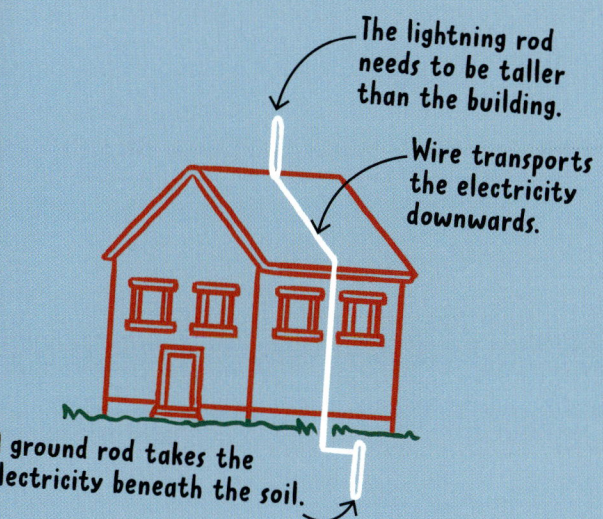

The lightning rod needs to be taller than the building.

Wire transports the electricity downwards.

A ground rod takes the electricity beneath the soil.

THE FLOW OF ELECTRICITY

Electricity sparked the curiosity of the ancient Egyptians, but it was not until the 1800s that scientists began to harness this power. Here are some of the key moments in the history of electrical energy.

THE FIRST MOTOR

English scientist Michael Faraday was the first to transform electricity into movement. He used a battery to create an electrical current through a wire, which made it move in the magnetic field around a magnet.

Copper wire was suspended over a glass with a magnet at the bottom.

2750 BC

NATURAL ELECTRICITY

Ancient Egyptians knew electric catfish in the Nile stunned their prey with electricity. The fish could survive out of water for a while and local medics used them to treat arthritis (but only with small catfish – bigger fish produced 350 volts!).

1821 → **1844**

MORSE CODE

American inventor Samuel Morse invented a telegraph machine which sent messages using electrical pulses. Each long or short pulse, or combination of pulses, translated to a letter.

ELECTRIC BATTERY

Italian scientist Alessandro Volta created the first battery. He layered discs of different metals, separated with paper soaked in salt water, for electricity to flow through. The "volt" unit of measurement was named after him.

1800

The key was pressed down to send a pulse of electricity.

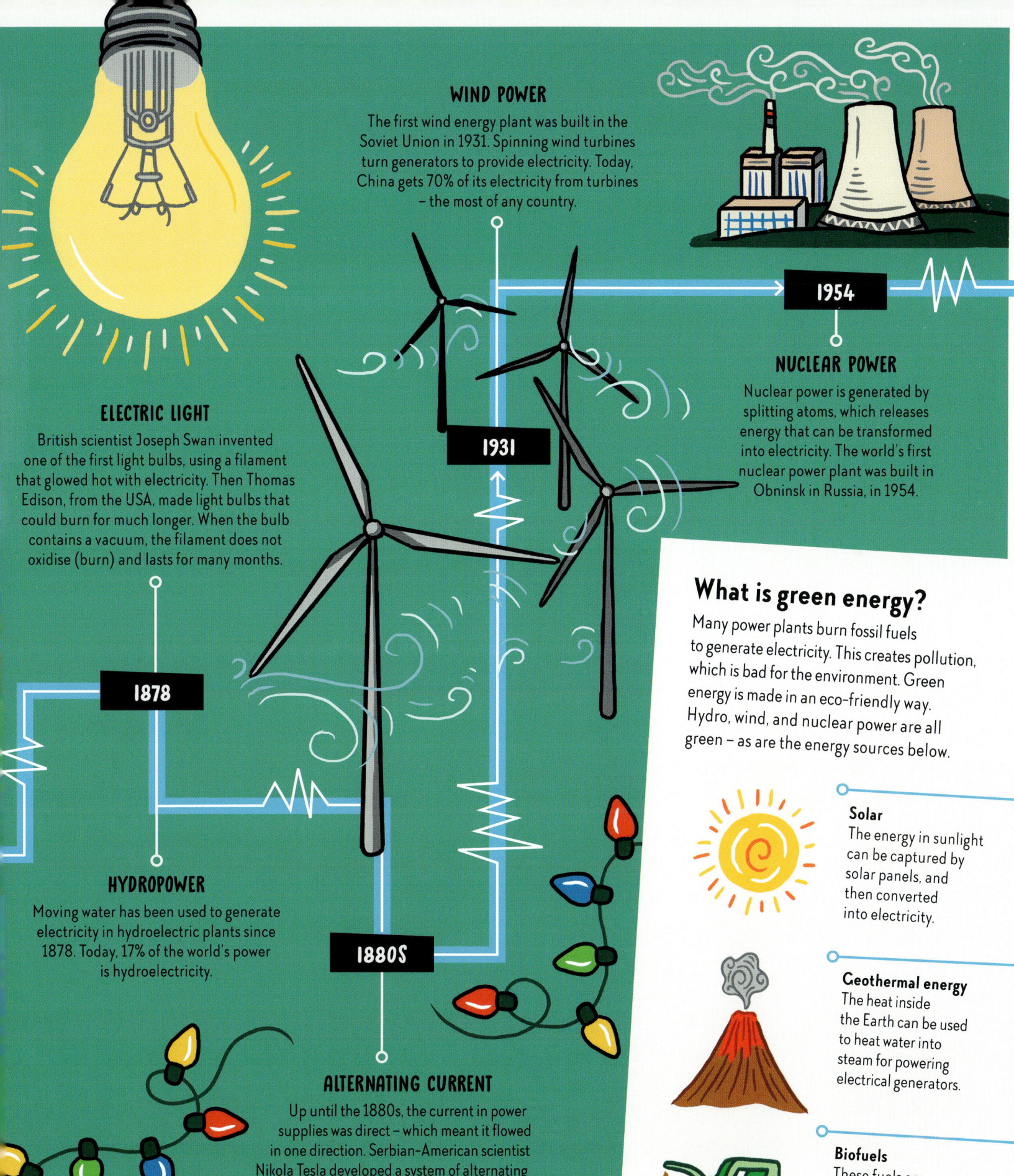

WIND POWER

The first wind energy plant was built in the Soviet Union in 1931. Spinning wind turbines turn generators to provide electricity. Today, China gets 70% of its electricity from turbines – the most of any country.

1954

NUCLEAR POWER

Nuclear power is generated by splitting atoms, which releases energy that can be transformed into electricity. The world's first nuclear power plant was built in Obninsk in Russia, in 1954.

ELECTRIC LIGHT

British scientist Joseph Swan invented one of the first light bulbs, using a filament that glowed hot with electricity. Then Thomas Edison, from the USA, made light bulbs that could burn for much longer. When the bulb contains a vacuum, the filament does not oxidise (burn) and lasts for many months.

1931

1878

HYDROPOWER

Moving water has been used to generate electricity in hydroelectric plants since 1878. Today, 17% of the world's power is hydroelectricity.

1880S

ALTERNATING CURRENT

Up until the 1880s, the current in power supplies was direct – which meant it flowed in one direction. Serbian-American scientist Nikola Tesla developed a system of alternating current (AC), which flowed in alternating directions. This system, still used today, worked better.

What is green energy?

Many power plants burn fossil fuels to generate electricity. This creates pollution, which is bad for the environment. Green energy is made in an eco-friendly way. Hydro, wind, and nuclear power are all green – as are the energy sources below.

Solar
The energy in sunlight can be captured by solar panels, and then converted into electricity.

Geothermal energy
The heat inside the Earth can be used to heat water into steam for powering electrical generators.

Biofuels
These fuels are made from organic matter. They produce less harmful pollution than fossil fuels.

What came before?

In the last 400 years or so, rich people often had their big houses and gardens fitted with ice caves. The ice could then be used to keep food cool all year round. But finding ice to put in the cave was not an easy task, and it often meant sending people to a distant mountain.

Gathering ice
High-up places, such as the tops of mountains, can be cold even when the surrounding areas are warm, so ice could be cut here.

Ice transportation
The ice had to be transported quickly, so that it did not melt, in covered carts that protected it from the heat of the Sun.

Ice storage
Ice caves might be built into a cool, shady area, under an earth mound.

REFRIGERATION

The science of keeping things cool helped stop food waste.

In warm temperatures, bacteria thrive on edible things – and these microbes can cause illnesses. Even before people knew about bacteria, they saw that food went rotten quickly as it was broken down by bacteria in hot weather. So, keeping food cool became vital.

From around 2000 BCE, people built storehouses with thick walls and used underground spaces that protected ice and food from the hot Sun. Hot air rises, and so some people made holes at the tops of storehouses to let warm air escape. From 400 BCE, ice houses called yakhchāls in Persia (in what is now Iran) took advantage of evaporation – when a liquid is heated to become a gas. Water vapour on the walls of these structures evaporated in the Sun. The evaporating particles used up energy from the warm surface, leaving it cooler.

Then, in 1834, The US inventor Jacob Perkins built a clever machine – the refrigerator. The machine used evaporation, like yakhchāls, but created a much more powerful cooling effect than is found in nature.

A yakhchāl

How does it work?

In coils on the outside the refrigerator, a special substance called a refrigerant cools from a vapour into a liquid. The liquid flows into the refrigerator, where the pressure is quickly lowered. Some of the liquid turns into gas, taking energy from the surrounding liquid and cooling it. The liquid then absorbs heat from the refrigerator, turns back into a vapour, and moves into the coils again.

The refrigerant moves around a circuit.

The first electric refrigerator small enough to fit in the home was invented in 1913, but refrigerators were not commonly found in homes until the 1950s.

What came next?

Transporting food

Without refrigeration, many types of food could not be transported because they would spoil on the journey. Now, we can transport food from other countries – which can be helpful if there is a local shortage of something.

Better health

We need vitamins and nutrients to stay healthy, and we get lots of these from fruit and vegetables. But these foods lose vitamins and nutrients as they age. Refrigerators keep the foods fresher for longer.

Many types of fruit last up to two weeks longer in a refrigerator.

Keeping medicines cool

Warm temperatures can cause medicines to change, so that they might not work as well in our bodies. Refrigerators are vital for keeping medicines at their most powerful.

113

CHAPTER 8

COMMUNICATION

Talking to each other, or reading each other's words in books, is essential for all scientists. Otherwise, we'd be making it up as we went along! Communication helps us to learn everything there is to know about our topic so that we can become an expert and make new discoveries. But it wasn't always easy to communicate.

For thousands of years, books had to be handwritten or hand stamped with letters or characters, which took a very long time! Very few copies of books would be made, so only a lucky few people could educate themselves and become scientists. The printing press changed all of that.

But there was still the problem of communicating directly with each other. Hand-delivered letters took days, weeks, or even months to arrive. Finally, in the 1800s, two inventions made instant communication possible – the telegraph and the radio.

GUTENBERG'S PRINTING PRESS

With the help of a brilliant goldsmith, books went from rare to everywhere.

The first book mass-produced with Gutenberg's printing press was the Bible.

Different methods of printing already existed before the printing press, but Gutenberg made it cheaper and easier.

Some old printing methods involved carving words, images, or whole pages into blocks of wood. These were covered with ink and pressed onto paper or animal skin. Carving the wood was time consuming and different books needed their own blocks. So, for many centuries, books were mostly handwritten, with few copies.

But in the 15th century, German inventor Johannes Gutenberg used his experience as a goldsmith to make large quantities of single letter blocks carved from metal. These stamps could be moved to spell out different words and reused for different books. Gutenberg's movable type could be used inside a machine called a printing press to make many copies of a book, quickly and easily.

Gutenberg's ink was innovative, too. It contained carbon particles for blackness and copper, lead, and titanium to make the surface glitter.

How did it work?

Printing words on paper required a machine called a printing press, or just press. Metal stamps of movable type were arranged to form sentences on a wooden plate. Leather pads were then used to transfer ink evenly onto the letters. Next, paper would be laid over the letters. Finally, a lever was operated to push the paper and inked words together.

Movable type

lever

Wooden plate

Paper

116

What next?

Sharing news

Gutenberg's version of the printing press spread across the world. More books were printed, and new types of printed products were invented, such as newspapers. People could find out what was going on – and protest if they were not happy about it.

Different languages

Before Gutenberg's printing press, almost all books in Europe were written in the ancient language of Latin, which was not well known to most people. More books meant texts were printed in other languages, too, so more people could read them.

Paper

Ink applicator

Sharing science

Scientific ideas were spread more easily. Scientists could share the results of their experiments. Printed copies of books were more likely to be correct than handwritten copies, because people couldn't accidentally write the wrong word, or add spelling mistakes.

GUTENBERG'S PRINTING PRESS

THE EVOLUTION OF PRINTING

Words and pictures have been printed for thousands of years, but the method and equipment we use have improved over time. Here are some of the inventions that have helped make printed pages more accessible.

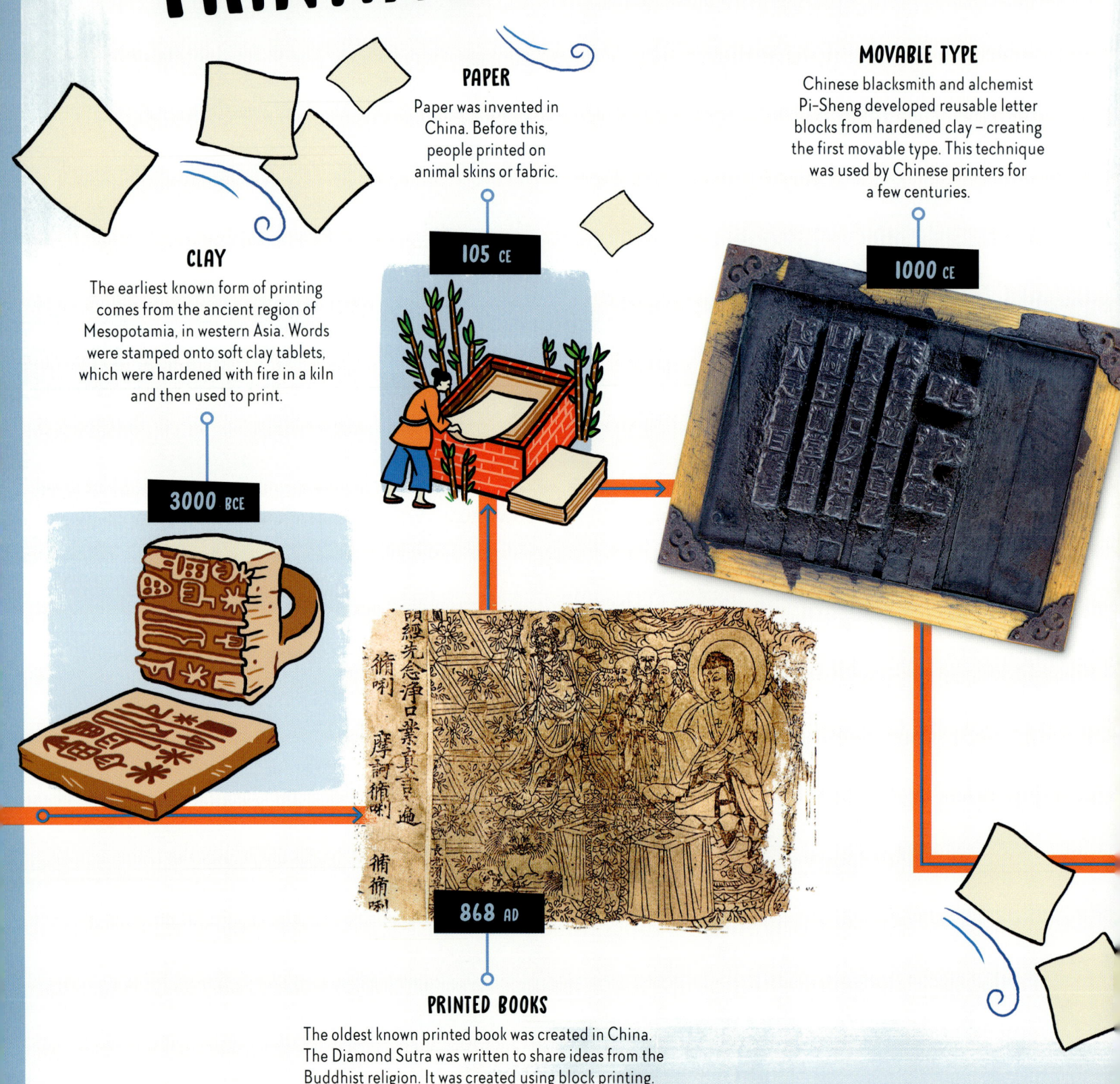

PAPER

Paper was invented in China. Before this, people printed on animal skins or fabric.

105 CE

MOVABLE TYPE

Chinese blacksmith and alchemist Pi-Sheng developed reusable letter blocks from hardened clay – creating the first movable type. This technique was used by Chinese printers for a few centuries.

1000 CE

CLAY

The earliest known form of printing comes from the ancient region of Mesopotamia, in western Asia. Words were stamped onto soft clay tablets, which were hardened with fire in a kiln and then used to print.

3000 BCE

PRINTED BOOKS

868 AD

The oldest known printed book was created in China. The Diamond Sutra was written to share ideas from the Buddhist religion. It was created using block printing.

GUTENBERG'S PRINTING PRESS

This press had movable metal type, which could be quickly rearranged into new text.

1455

STEAM-POWERED PRINTING PRESS

Richard M. Hoe from the USA made the first steam-powered printing press. People no longer needed to operate the printing press by hand.

1800

1843

IRON PRINTING PRESS

British scientist Lord Stanhope built a printing press made from cast iron. With this heavy material, it took less physical effort to make a print.

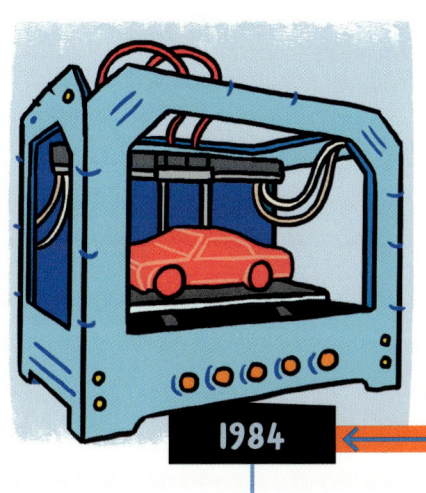

1984

1969

3D PRINTING

Chuck Hull, an engineer from the USA, invented the first 3D printer. It could print objects, not just flat pages!

LASER PRINTING

The laser printer was invented by Gary Starkweather from the USA. Letter blocks were no longer needed with this machine, so printers could be a lot smaller.

1377

METAL TYPE

The oldest known book using metal block printing was made in Korea. It included ideas from Buddhism and important Korean thinkers.

Printing speeds

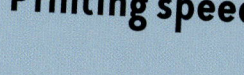

By hand
2–4 pages per hour

Gutenberg's printing press
25 pages per hour

Steam-powered printing press
1,100 pages per hour

Laser printers
12,000 pages per hour

COOKE AND WHEATSTONE'S TELEGRAPH

THE TELEGRAPH

The telegraph began the era of instant long-distance communication.

At the start of the 1800s it could take days or weeks to send messages between cities. The words had to be written out on paper and carried by post. But in the first half of the century, on either side of the Atlantic ocean, twin inventions were built that would change how we communicate.

An electric telegraph invented by British team William Fothergill Cooke and Charles Wheatstone was patented in 1837. It used wires and pulses of electricity to spell out a message on a receiver. At the same time, in the USA, Samuel Morse was working on his own electrical messaging machine. His telegraph would send its first message in 1844.

Quick communication was useful in many ways. Cooke and Wheatstone's machine helped people catch a murderer escaping by train, when a message was sent ahead to the station for which he was bound. During the US Civil War, from 1861 to 1865, the telegraph was used to share news and to give instructions. The device also helped friends and families who lived apart to stay in touch.

Telegraph lines were set up across land and beneath the sea. The first transatlantic cable, connecting Canada and Ireland, was laid in 1858.

How did Cooke and Wheatstone's telegraph work?

Cooke and Wheatstone developed a system with five metallic needles, which could be moved using an electric current. The current was used to point the needles at different letters and numbers on a panel. The panel did not have the letters "Q" or "J", which caused some confusion when sending early messages!

Letters on a panel
Here, the two outer needles are pointing to the letter "A". The other needles are stationary.

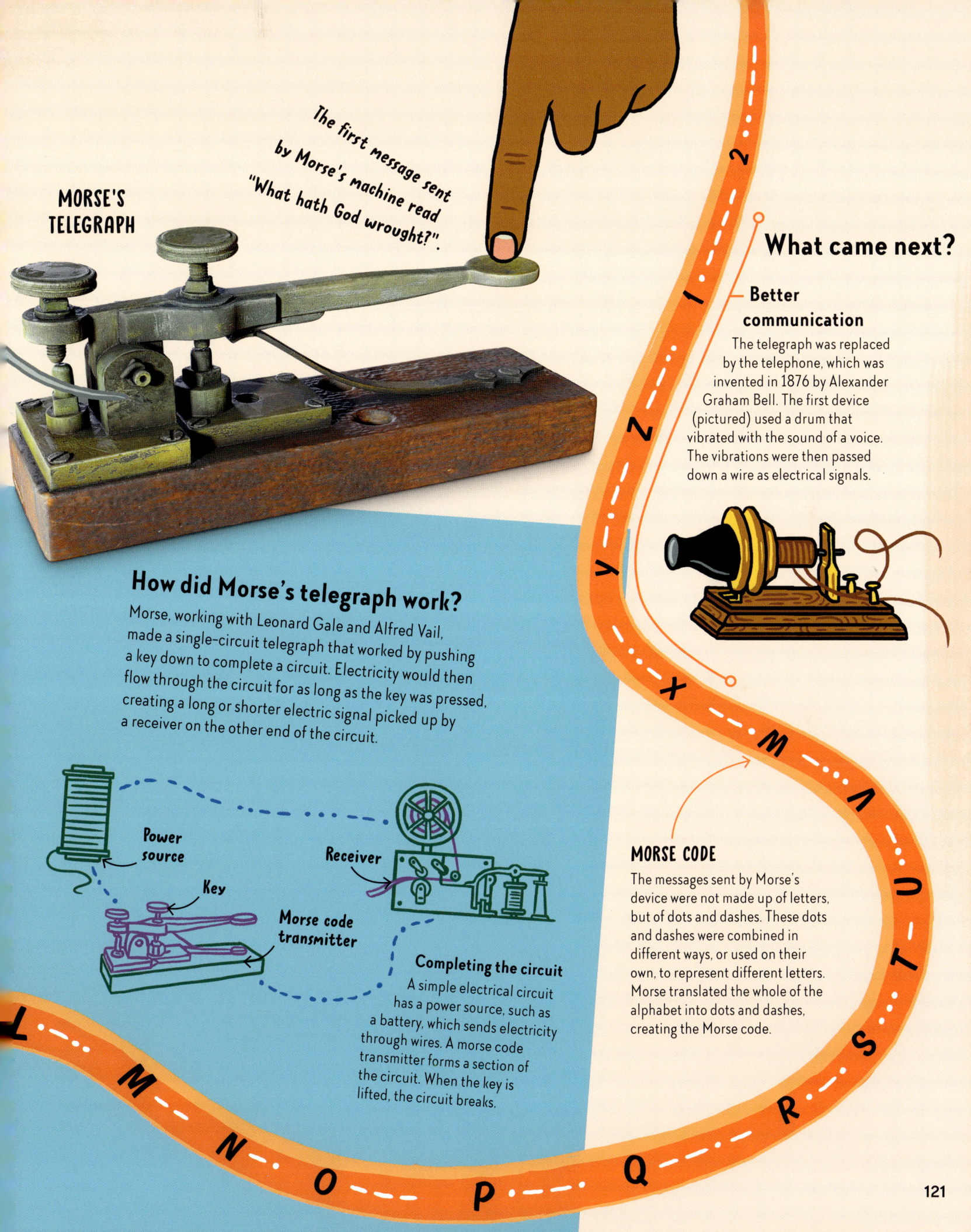

MORSE'S TELEGRAPH

The first message sent by Morse's machine read "What hath God wrought?".

How did Morse's telegraph work?

Morse, working with Leonard Gale and Alfred Vail, made a single-circuit telegraph that worked by pushing a key down to complete a circuit. Electricity would then flow through the circuit for as long as the key was pressed, creating a long or shorter electric signal picked up by a receiver on the other end of the circuit.

Power source

Key

Receiver

Morse code transmitter

Completing the circuit

A simple electrical circuit has a power source, such as a battery, which sends electricity through wires. A morse code transmitter forms a section of the circuit. When the key is lifted, the circuit breaks.

What came next?

Better communication

The telegraph was replaced by the telephone, which was invented in 1876 by Alexander Graham Bell. The first device (pictured) used a drum that vibrated with the sound of a voice. The vibrations were then passed down a wire as electrical signals.

MORSE CODE

The messages sent by Morse's device were not made up of letters, but of dots and dashes. These dots and dashes were combined in different ways, or used on their own, to represent different letters. Morse translated the whole of the alphabet into dots and dashes, creating the Morse code.

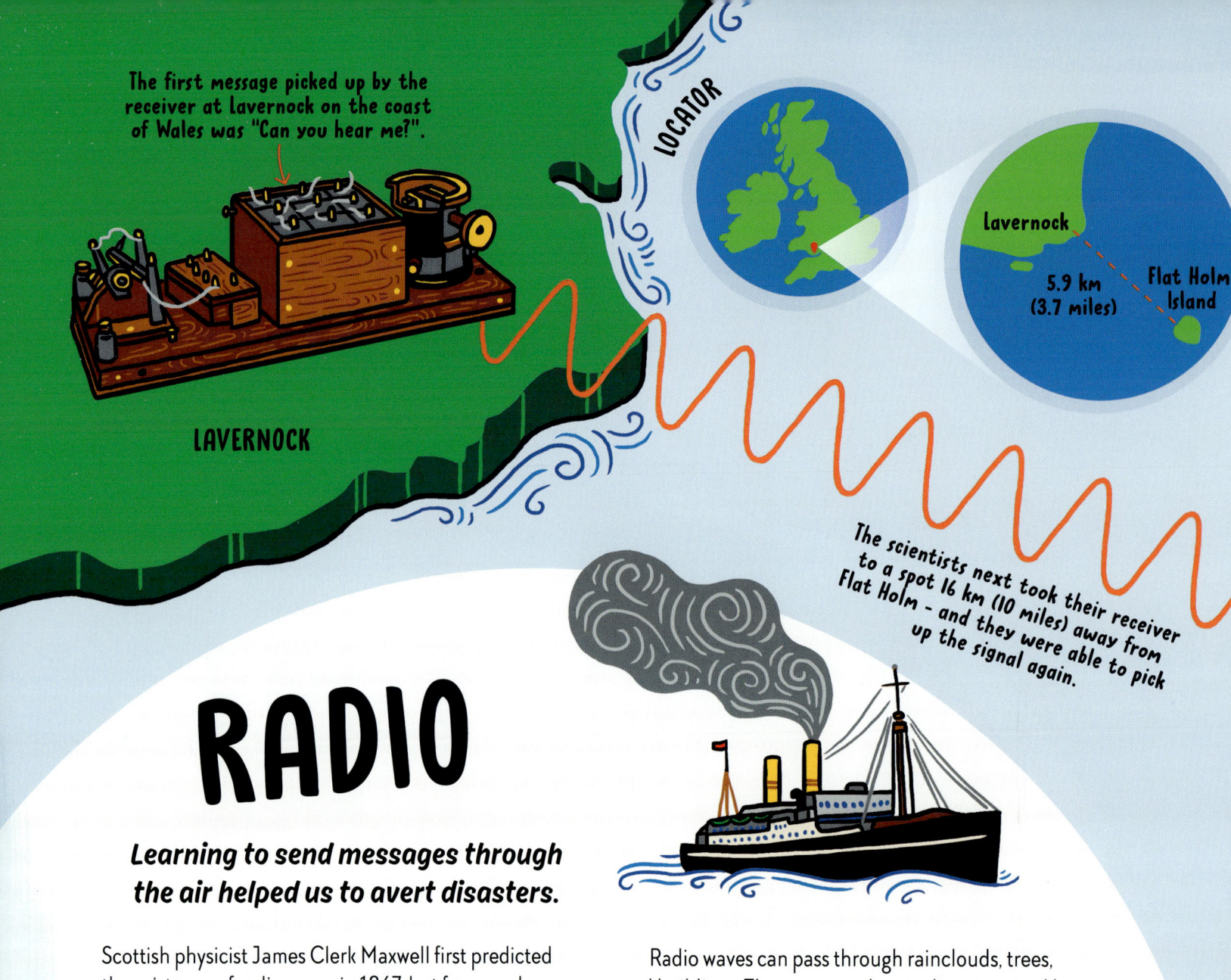

The first message picked up by the receiver at Lavernock on the coast of Wales was "Can you hear me?".

LAVERNOCK

LOCATOR

Lavernock

5.9 km (3.7 miles)

Flat Holm Island

The scientists next took their receiver to a spot 16 km (10 miles) away from Flat Holm – and they were able to pick up the signal again.

RADIO

Learning to send messages through the air helped us to avert disasters.

Scottish physicist James Clerk Maxwell first predicted the existence of radio waves in 1867, but few people other than scientists were interested in his idea. Maxwell described the waves as unseen light, moving through space. It would take another 28 years for the Italian inventor Guglielmo Marconi to show how useful this new discovery could be.

Marconi invented a working radio transmitter and receiver, which sent and received the first radio signal in 1895. The device worked by sending waves in shorter and longer bursts, which could be used to send Morse code – a code that turns short and long sounds into letters. Being able to send messages through the air meant that people could communicate almost anywhere, even at sea. Marconi proved this when he sent the first radio message over open water in 1897, from Flat Holm Island to Lavernock in the UK. Four years later, in 1901, the first trans-Atlantic wireless transmission was made.

Radio waves can pass through rainclouds, trees, and buildings. They can travel great distances, and be reflected or bent over hills and mountains, to beyond the horizon. And once we knew how to send sounds using radio waves, we could learn how to send images and much more.

How do radio waves carry sounds?

The number of times that a wave repeats in a second is called its frequency. Like radio waves, sound travels in waves. Frequency modulation (FM) transmitters receive sound waves through a microphone and change the frequency of radio waves to match them. These radio waves then carry the sound.

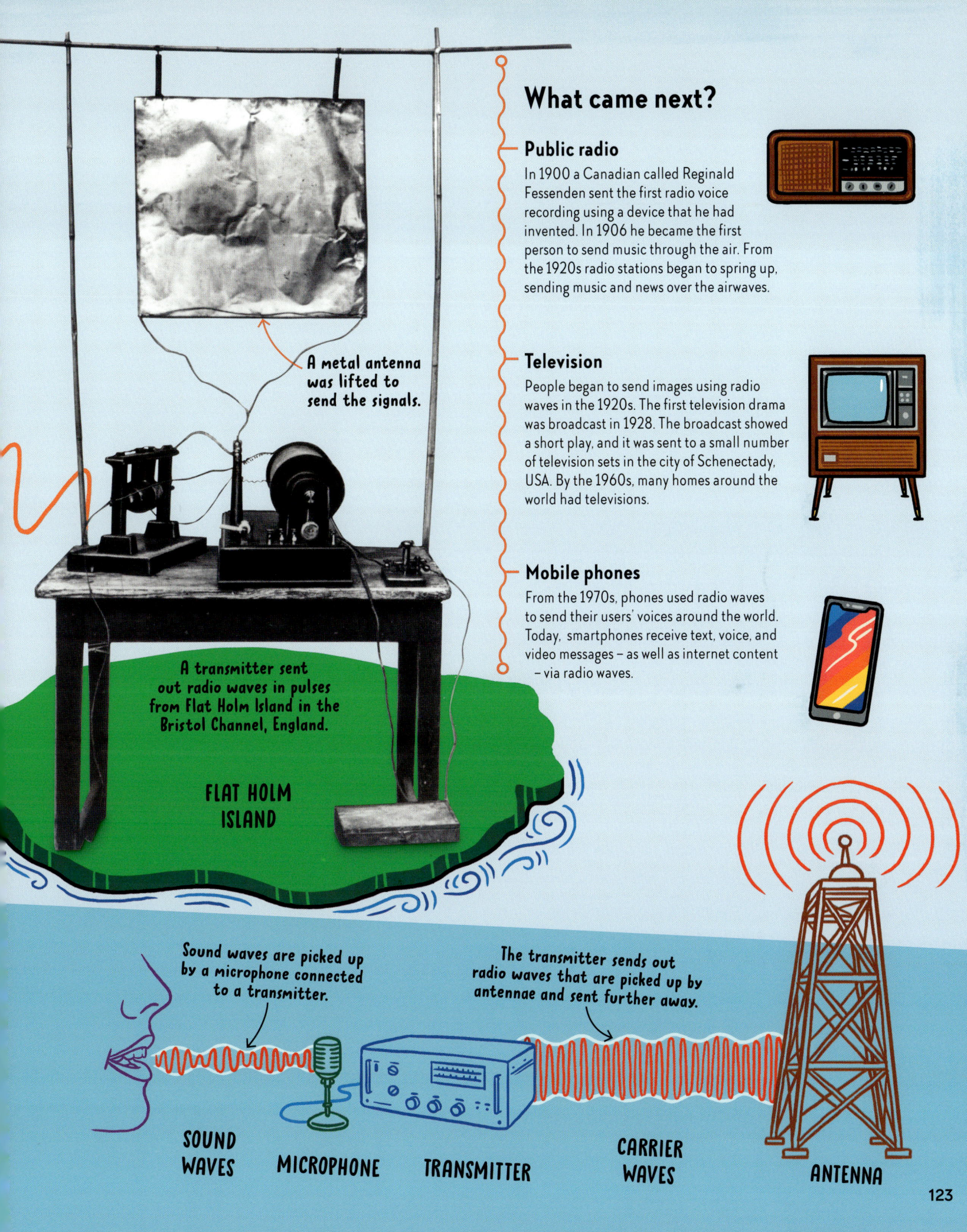

A metal antenna was lifted to send the signals.

What came next?

Public radio

In 1900 a Canadian called Reginald Fessenden sent the first radio voice recording using a device that he had invented. In 1906 he became the first person to send music through the air. From the 1920s radio stations began to spring up, sending music and news over the airwaves.

Television

People began to send images using radio waves in the 1920s. The first television drama was broadcast in 1928. The broadcast showed a short play, and it was sent to a small number of television sets in the city of Schenectady, USA. By the 1960s, many homes around the world had televisions.

Mobile phones

From the 1970s, phones used radio waves to send their users' voices around the world. Today, smartphones receive text, voice, and video messages – as well as internet content – via radio waves.

A transmitter sent out radio waves in pulses from Flat Holm Island in the Bristol Channel, England.

FLAT HOLM ISLAND

Sound waves are picked up by a microphone connected to a transmitter.

The transmitter sends out radio waves that are picked up by antennae and sent further away.

SOUND WAVES **MICROPHONE** **TRANSMITTER** **CARRIER WAVES** **ANTENNA**

CHAPTER 9

HEALTHCARE

It is difficult to choose great medical breakthroughs. Records can be lost over time. Hippocrates from ancient Greece is one of the most famous physicians in history, but his written work was destroyed after his death. And not all great modern discoveries win Nobel Prizes. Most improvements in medical treatments are made one step at a time, by many pioneers working in different places during different historical periods. So, the breakthroughs in this chapter are just a small part of the story of healthcare. But they have all made a big difference to people's lives.

The science of clean water helps stop the spread of some diseases. Vaccines brought the Covid pandemic under control and MRI scanners help doctors to see what's going on inside patients. Psychiatry helps millions of people with mental health problems and IVF allows people to have children who couldn't have them otherwise.

MODERN MEDICINE

Hospitals are full of amazing scientific discoveries and inventions from the last few hundred years. These advancements help us to understand how illnesses are caused, to diagnose problems with the body, and to cure patients.

1861

GERM THEORY

Dutch scientist Antonie van Leeuwenhoek first spotted tiny living things under a microscope in the mid-1600s. But it wasn't until 1861 that French scientist Louis Pasteur wrote that microscopic creatures, or germs, cause diseases.

1796

THE FIRST VACCINE

To prevent a patient from falling ill with smallpox, an English doctor called Edward Jenner infected the patient with cowpox – a similar, but milder, disease. The patient developed an immune response to cowpox, which means their body could fight it off. The immune response also worked for smallpox.

1844

ANAESTHESIA

Operations were once done without numbing the patient or putting them to sleep, which is what anaesthesia does today. Anaesthesia was invented in 1844, when a dentist first administered a pain-numbing gas, called nitrous oxide, during a procedure.

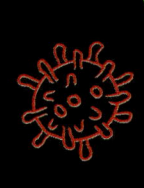

1829

WATER PURIFCATION

The first system for treating, or cleaning, public water was put in place in 1829, at the Chelsea Waterworks Company in London, UK. Sand was used to catch particles of dirt, which helped stop waterborne diseases from spreading (though people did not know why at the time).

The discovery of antibiotics happened by chance, when a mould found its way into a petri dish in a lab.

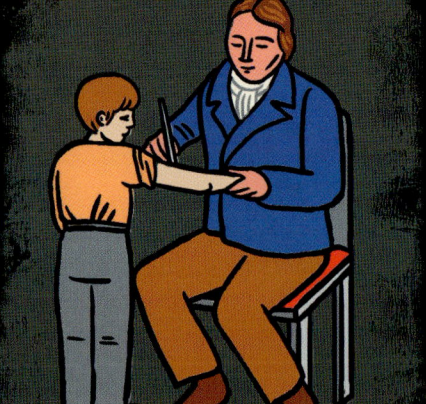

X-RAYS

German scientist W.C. Röntgen discovered that a type of radiation could be used to take pictures of bones inside the body. The rays passed through skin but could not easily pass through bone, which created a shadow on special paper.

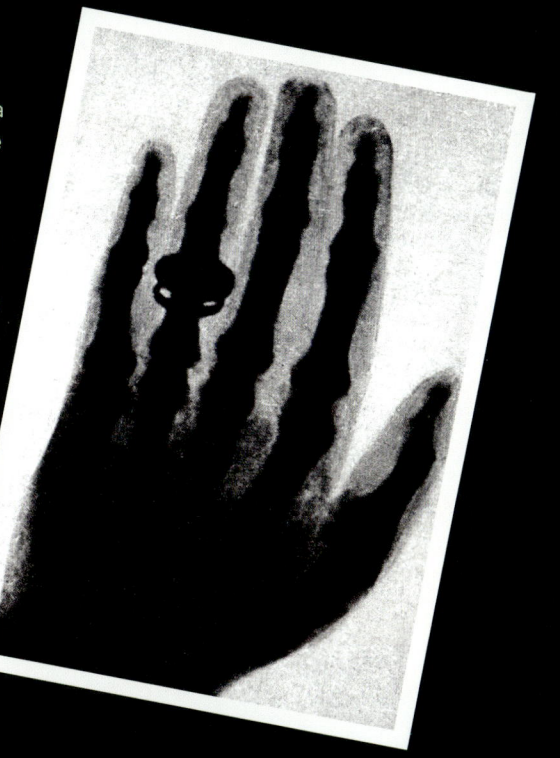

1895

LAB-GROWN BODY PARTS

In 1998, scientists discovered how to grow human stem cells in the lab. Some stem cells can become any type of body part. We have since used them to grow skin and other organs.

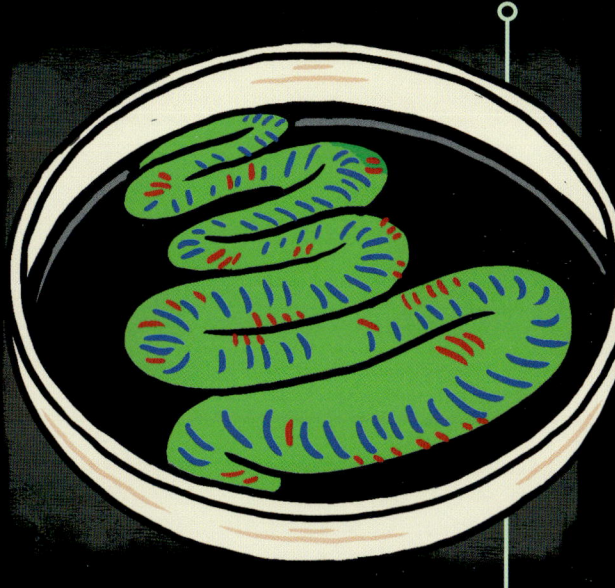

1928

ANTIBIOTICS

Scottish scientist Alexander Fleming was the first to notice that penicillin (a type of mould) killed germs in a petri dish. Today, penicillin is one of hundreds of antibiotics that can fight off bacterial infections in patients.

1954

THE FIRST TRANSPLANT

A kidney was the first organ to be successfully transplanted from one person to another. The first heart transplant took place in 1967.

1990

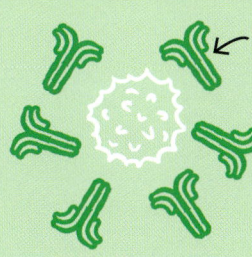

GENE THERAPY

Doctors were first able to successfully treat a patient using a gene that they had coded in the lab in 1990. The patient had not been able to fight off diseases, but the gene gave her that ability.

1998

How vaccines work

Virus

White blood cell

Antibodies

1. Scientists create a harmless version of a virus, part of the virus, or its genetic code.

2. The harmless version is injected into the bloodstream, where it is met by white blood cells.

3. White blood cells develop antibodies to fight off the harmless version.

4. If you are exposed to the virus, your body knows how to make antibodies to destroy it.

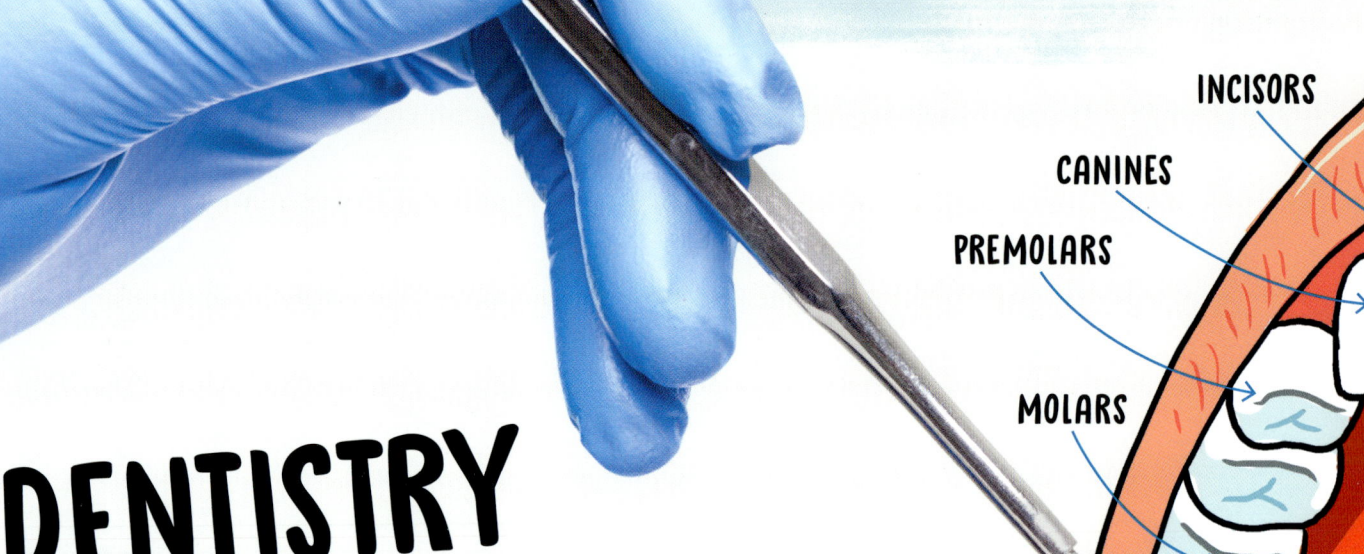

DENTISTRY

Toothache has inspired ingenious treatments and tools.

Archaeologists have discovered teeth with fillings made around 13,000 years ago, in Italy. A stone tool was used to scrape out tooth decay from a cavity (hole) in the tooth, and a sticky, black, natural tar, called bitumen, was used to fill the hole.

Though Stone Age people had cavities to treat, it's unlikely they knew what caused tooth decay. It wasn't until the 1600s that French doctor Pierre Fauchard linked eating sugar to cavities. Cavities were far more common at this time than in the past. Sugar reached Europe from West Asia in around the 11th century, and it began to be grown in large amounts in the 1500s. Then, in the 1890s, American dentist, and the world's first oral biologist, Willoughby D. Miller said that bacteria causes tooth decay. But which is it? Well, the answer is both – bacteria eat sugar in the mouth and then produce acid, which wears away the tooth.

Since discovering the causes of tooth decay, much has been done to try to stop it. Beginning in the mid-1900s, some countries around the world, such as the USA, began adding fluorides (usually sodium fluoride) to drinking water in tiny amounts. These chemicals help keep the dentine in teeth strong. And, to get rid of food that bacteria could feed on, it's very important to brush your teeth!

What's inside a tooth?

The visible part of a tooth is the strong, white enamel that coats it. Inside is the soft pulp, and inside that are nerves – which send pain signals to your brain when you have toothache. Beneath your gum is the V-shaped root, which anchors the tooth in place.

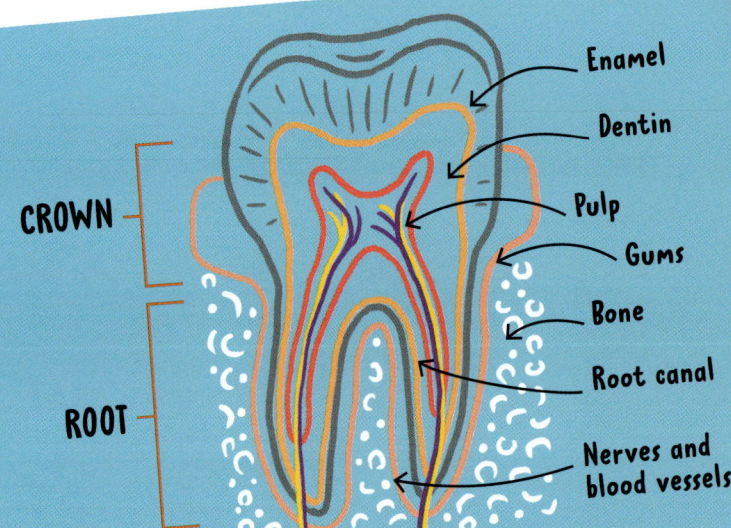

CROWN

ROOT

Enamel

Dentin

Pulp

Gums

Bone

Root canal

Nerves and blood vessels

AHHHHHH

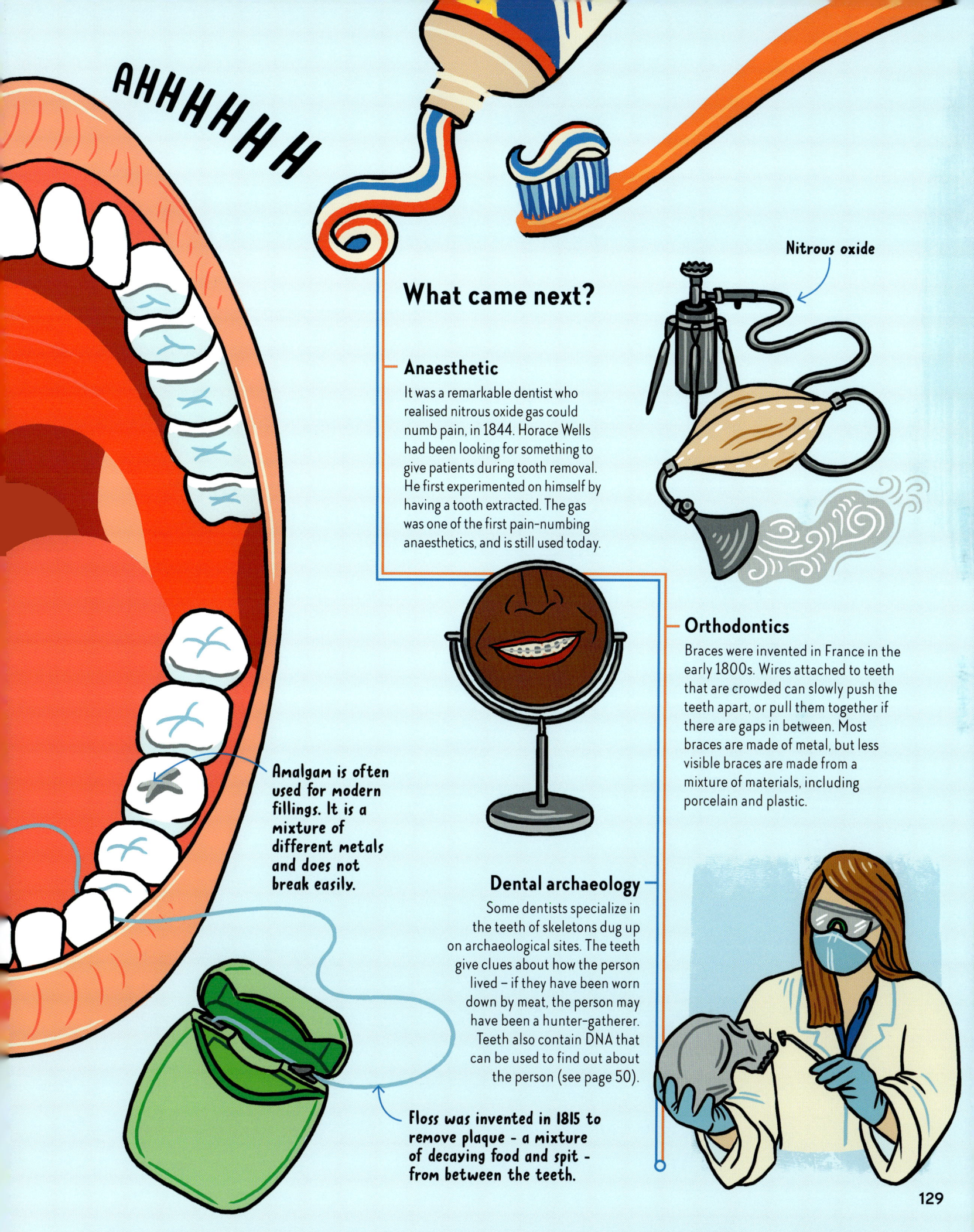

Nitrous oxide

What came next?

Anaesthetic

It was a remarkable dentist who realised nitrous oxide gas could numb pain, in 1844. Horace Wells had been looking for something to give patients during tooth removal. He first experimented on himself by having a tooth extracted. The gas was one of the first pain-numbing anaesthetics, and is still used today.

Orthodontics

Braces were invented in France in the early 1800s. Wires attached to teeth that are crowded can slowly push the teeth apart, or pull them together if there are gaps in between. Most braces are made of metal, but less visible braces are made from a mixture of materials, including porcelain and plastic.

Amalgam is often used for modern fillings. It is a mixture of different metals and does not break easily.

Dental archaeology

Some dentists specialize in the teeth of skeletons dug up on archaeological sites. The teeth give clues about how the person lived – if they have been worn down by meat, the person may have been a hunter-gatherer. Teeth also contain DNA that can be used to find out about the person (see page 50).

Floss was invented in 1815 to remove plaque - a mixture of decaying food and spit - from between the teeth.

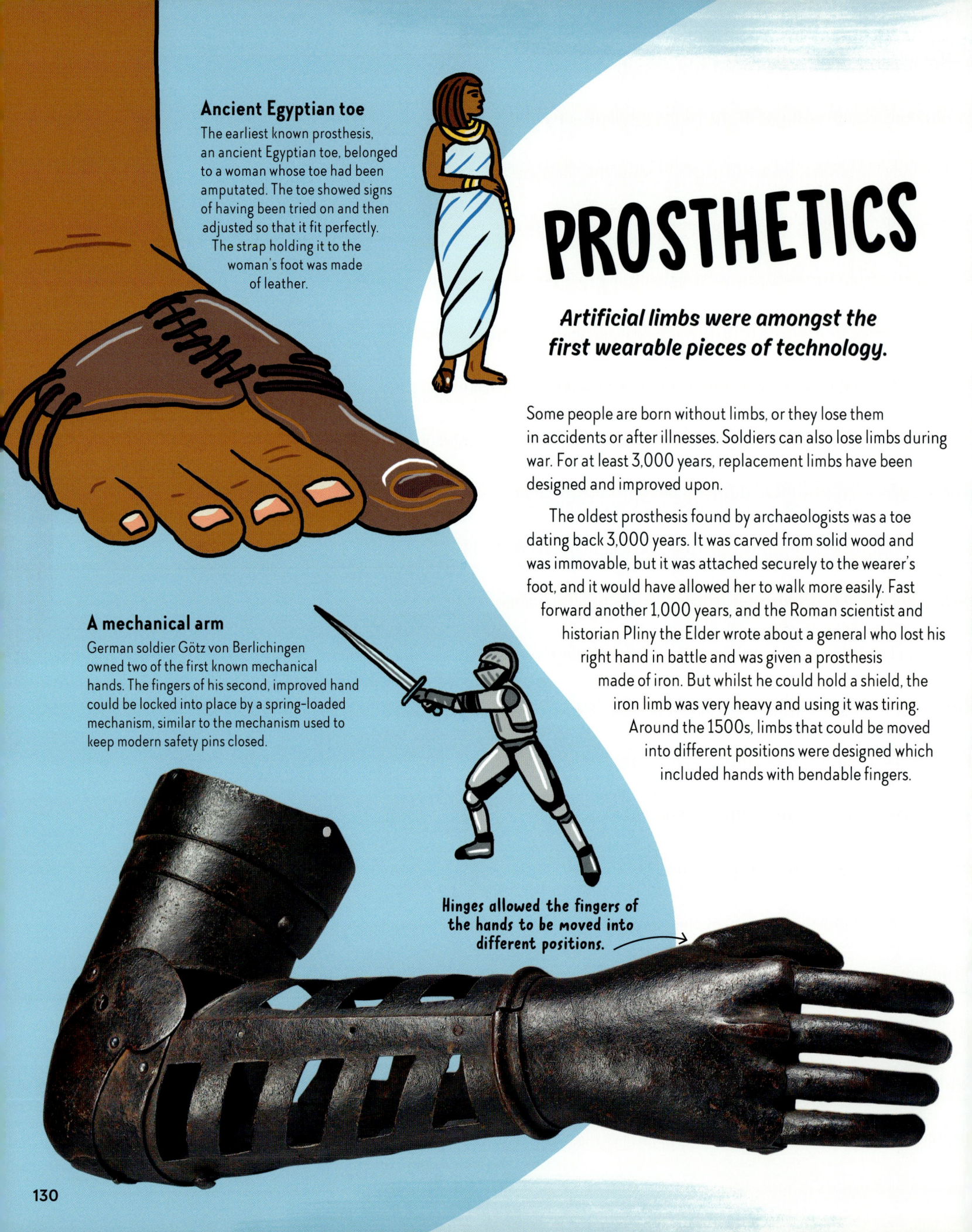

Ancient Egyptian toe

The earliest known prosthesis, an ancient Egyptian toe, belonged to a woman whose toe had been amputated. The toe showed signs of having been tried on and then adjusted so that it fit perfectly. The strap holding it to the woman's foot was made of leather.

PROSTHETICS

Artificial limbs were amongst the first wearable pieces of technology.

Some people are born without limbs, or they lose them in accidents or after illnesses. Soldiers can also lose limbs during war. For at least 3,000 years, replacement limbs have been designed and improved upon.

The oldest prosthesis found by archaeologists was a toe dating back 3,000 years. It was carved from solid wood and was immovable, but it was attached securely to the wearer's foot, and it would have allowed her to walk more easily. Fast forward another 1,000 years, and the Roman scientist and historian Pliny the Elder wrote about a general who lost his right hand in battle and was given a prosthesis made of iron. But whilst he could hold a shield, the iron limb was very heavy and using it was tiring. Around the 1500s, limbs that could be moved into different positions were designed which included hands with bendable fingers.

A mechanical arm

German soldier Götz von Berlichingen owned two of the first known mechanical hands. The fingers of his second, improved hand could be locked into place by a spring-loaded mechanism, similar to the mechanism used to keep modern safety pins closed.

Hinges allowed the fingers of the hands to be moved into different positions.

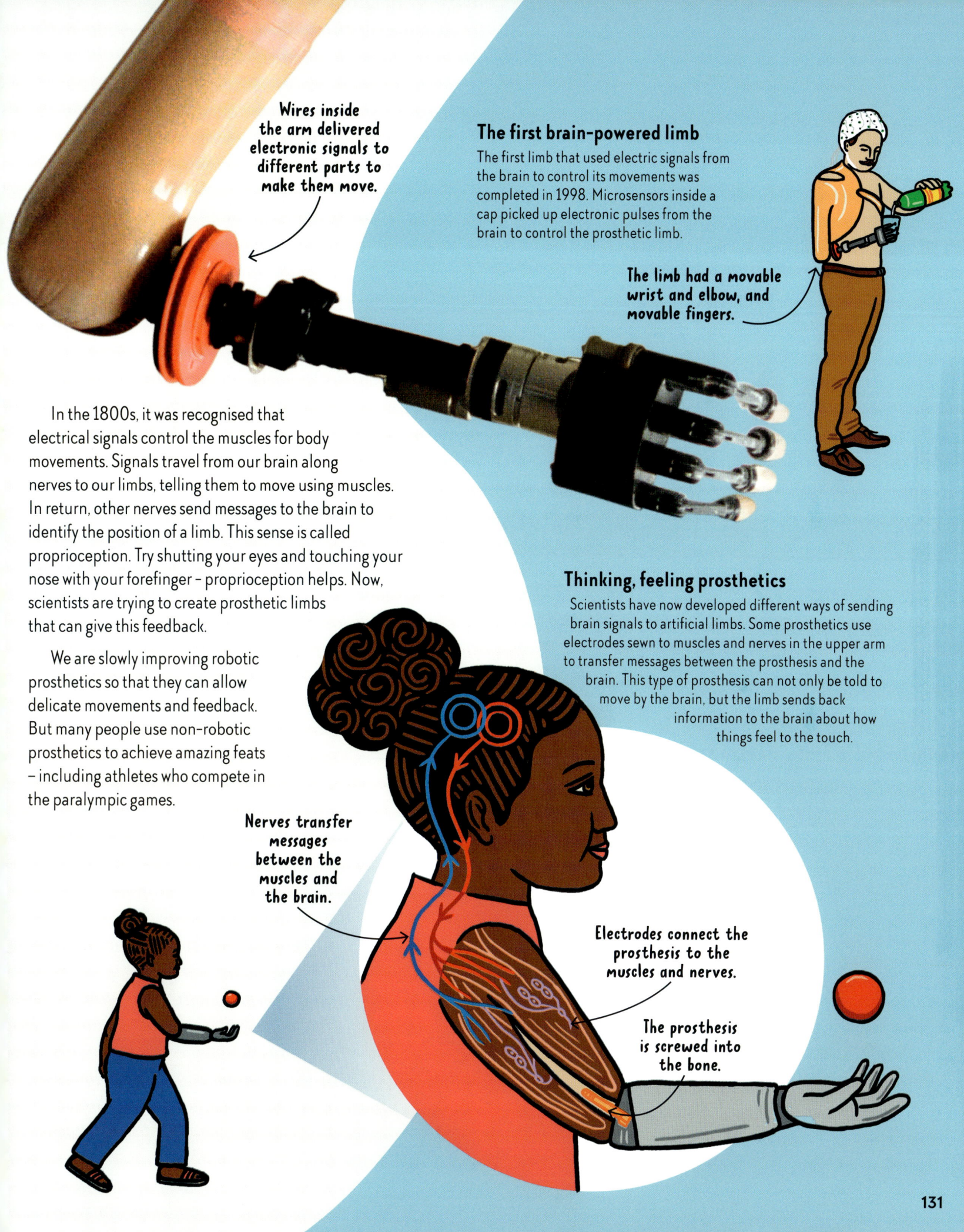

Wires inside the arm delivered electronic signals to different parts to make them move.

The first brain-powered limb

The first limb that used electric signals from the brain to control its movements was completed in 1998. Microsensors inside a cap picked up electronic pulses from the brain to control the prosthetic limb.

The limb had a movable wrist and elbow, and movable fingers.

In the 1800s, it was recognised that electrical signals control the muscles for body movements. Signals travel from our brain along nerves to our limbs, telling them to move using muscles. In return, other nerves send messages to the brain to identify the position of a limb. This sense is called proprioception. Try shutting your eyes and touching your nose with your forefinger - proprioception helps. Now, scientists are trying to create prosthetic limbs that can give this feedback.

We are slowly improving robotic prosthetics so that they can allow delicate movements and feedback. But many people use non-robotic prosthetics to achieve amazing feats – including athletes who compete in the paralympic games.

Thinking, feeling prosthetics

Scientists have now developed different ways of sending brain signals to artificial limbs. Some prosthetics use electrodes sewn to muscles and nerves in the upper arm to transfer messages between the prosthesis and the brain. This type of prosthesis can not only be told to move by the brain, but the limb sends back information to the brain about how things feel to the touch.

Nerves transfer messages between the muscles and the brain.

Electrodes connect the prosthesis to the muscles and nerves.

The prosthesis is screwed into the bone.

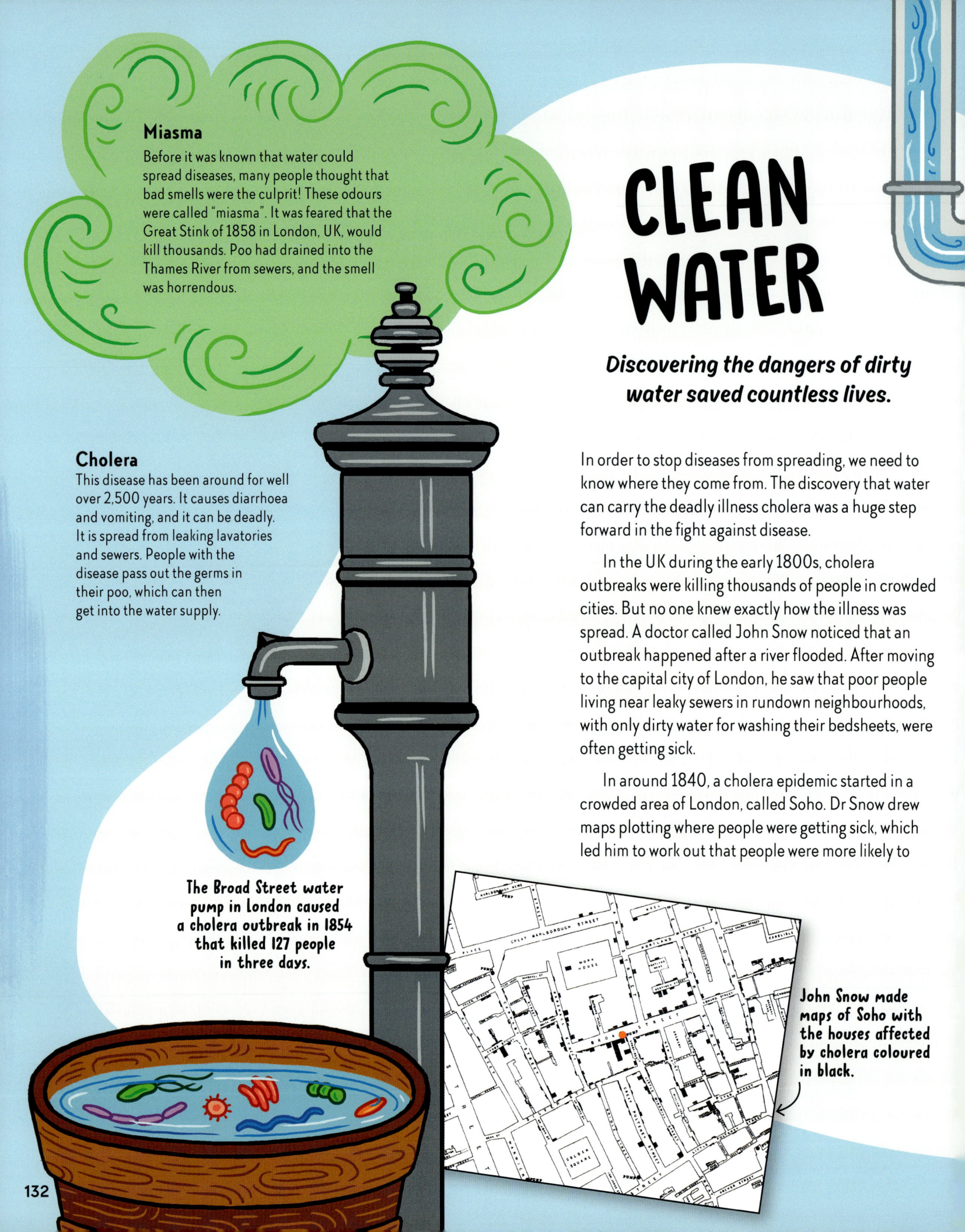

Miasma

Before it was known that water could spread diseases, many people thought that bad smells were the culprit! These odours were called "miasma". It was feared that the Great Stink of 1858 in London, UK, would kill thousands. Poo had drained into the Thames River from sewers, and the smell was horrendous.

Cholera

This disease has been around for well over 2,500 years. It causes diarrhoea and vomiting, and it can be deadly. It is spread from leaking lavatories and sewers. People with the disease pass out the germs in their poo, which can then get into the water supply.

The Broad Street water pump in London caused a cholera outbreak in 1854 that killed 127 people in three days.

CLEAN WATER

Discovering the dangers of dirty water saved countless lives.

In order to stop diseases from spreading, we need to know where they come from. The discovery that water can carry the deadly illness cholera was a huge step forward in the fight against disease.

In the UK during the early 1800s, cholera outbreaks were killing thousands of people in crowded cities. But no one knew exactly how the illness was spread. A doctor called John Snow noticed that an outbreak happened after a river flooded. After moving to the capital city of London, he saw that poor people living near leaky sewers in rundown neighbourhoods, with only dirty water for washing their bedsheets, were often getting sick.

In around 1840, a cholera epidemic started in a crowded area of London, called Soho. Dr Snow drew maps plotting where people were getting sick, which led him to work out that people were more likely to

John Snow made maps of Soho with the houses affected by cholera coloured in black.

Cleaning steps

Modern sewers transport dirty water to treatment plants, where the water is cleaned. This process has a number of clever steps.

Coagulation chemicals are added.

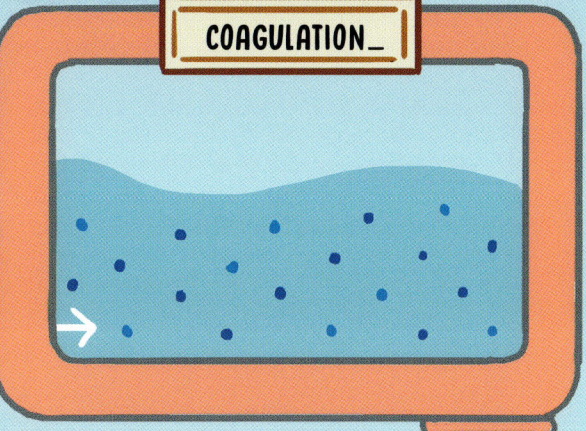

COAGULATION_

Chemicals added to the water lead particles of waste inside it to coagulate – which means they clump together to form larger particles.

Snow believed in the theory that diseases are tiny living things, called germs. We now know that this theory is true, but it was not widely believed at the time.

catch cholera if they drank water from a pump in Broad Street. He persuaded the local council to remove its handle. People grumbled about walking further to find water – but they stopped falling ill.

It was discovered that the pump water came from a well dug just 1 m (3 ft) away from a cesspit – a pit into which toilets drain. The cloth nappy of a baby with cholera had washed into the cesspit, which may have caused the outbreak.

It took some time for John Snow's findings about water and the spread of disease to be accepted. But eventually, governments and city planners began to build sewers that would carry waste further away from people's homes, and to find ways to clean the water before it was made available to drink. Today, John Snow is known as the father of epidemiology – the science of how diseases spread.

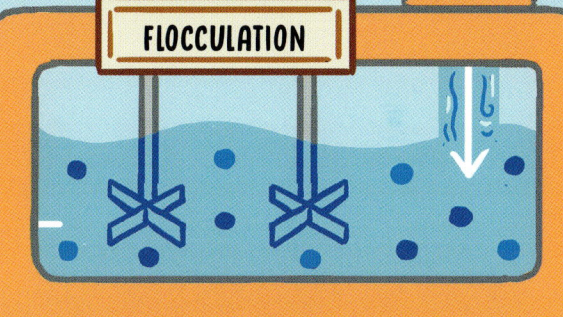

FLOCCULATION

Next, the water is gently mixed so that the clumps join together to form flakes. Chemicals can be added to help flakes form.

SEDIMENTATION

During this stage, heavy flakes of pollution sink to the bottom of the tank and form sediment.

Sometimes, chemicals are added, which kill any remaining germs.

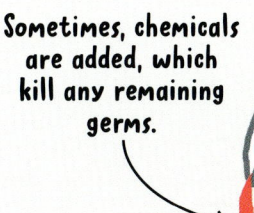

FILTRATION

The water then passes through layers of grainy materials, such as sand. Any remaining sediment is too big to flow through, so it is filtered out.

The four humours

From ancient Greece up until the 1700s, many people in Europe believed that there were four main fluids in the body, called humours, and that these needed to be perfectly balanced for someone to have good health. The fluids were phlegm (top left), blood (top right), yellow bile (bottom right), and black bile (bottom left). Too much of any of them would cause mental and bodily illness.

PSYCHIATRY

Hippocrates, the father of medicine, thought it was more important to treat the mind than the body.

Coined in 1808 by German physician Johann Christian Reil, the term "psychiatry" comes from Greek words meaning "medical treatment of the soul". But, by "soul", Reil actually meant the mind.

The earliest forms of psychiatry can be traced back to ancient Greece, Rome, and India. In ancient Greece, Hippocrates (460–377 BCE) classified mental illnesses into different disorders, each with their own set of symptoms, for perhaps the first time. He also wrote that problems with the mind

Air

Earth

Ayurveda

More than 5,000 years ago in India, people began to practise a way of thinking called Ayurveda. Practitioners believe that the five elements of air, earth, ether (space), fire, and water combine in different ways to form energies, called doshas, which exist inside people and affect their mental and bodily wellbeing.

Fire

Water

Space

may be caused by problems with the body. Still, up until the 1800s, many people thought that mental health conditions were caused by demons.

Dr. Benjamin Rush, the "father of American psychiatry", was one of the first of his age to believe that mental illness was a disease. He wrote the USA's earliest psychiatric textbook, which was printed in 1812. Towards the end of the 1800s, German psychiatrist Emil Kraepelin devised a better classification system for mental illnesses, including disorders that are still recognised today. Kraepelin also said that some mental illnesses were caused by a person's experiences, while others were because of problems with their body.

Gradually, psychiatrists learned more and more about mental disorders and their causes. Today, people suffering from many of these illnesses can be successfully treated with therapy or medication.

In the early 1800s, some people thought that personality traits were linked to bumps on the skull, where the brain underneath had changed shape. Called phrenology, this was definitely not true!

Releasing emotions

In ancient Greece, people with physical and mental illnesses were sometimes told to listen to music or to go to the theatre as treatment. During plays about tragedies, a person's emotions would be affected by the story on stage. This was thought to allow them to release their own emotions.

Mental health hospitals

One of the earliest hospitals for mental health was built in Baghdad, Iraq, in 792. Bethlem hospital (pictured) in London, UK, may have been treating people with mental illnesses from as early as the 1300s. Also called "Bedlam", it became known for its cruel treatment of patients. Gradually, from the late-1700s, mental health hospitals were built with the aim of treating patients with care and respect.

Where we are now

Since the early 1900s, psychotherapy has become a popular method for treating many mental illnesses. Medications have existed since the 1950s. Much more recently there have been attempts to understand the complex nature of mental ill health. Being able to make images of the brain (such as MRI images) is a major advance. And we are learning how genes and hormones in the brain affect mental health.

The frog's sperm was used to fertilize the eggs.

The first IVF

In c.1770, scientist called Lazzaro Spallanzani made little silk shorts for the male frogs in his pond. When he took the shorts off, there was fluid on the inside – sperm. He dropped the fluid into his pond alongside a female frog's eggs. The eggs grew into tadpoles – the first IVF babies.

A zygote is a fertilized egg. It forms when the nuclei of an egg and a sperm fuse, then divide into two.

ZYGOTE

Making mammals

Min Chueh Chang took eggs from a black rabbit and added sperm to fertilize them. He kept the eggs warm in an insulator and injected them into the womb of a white rabbit. She then gave birth to the first IVF mammals.

The white rabbit gave birth to black babies - proving they were from the IVF.

IVF

Growing babies in the laboratory changed the lives of people who couldn't have children.

In the 1660s, people began to realise that babies are formed when a sperm from a male animal meets the egg of a female. In vitro fertilization (IVF) involves mixing a sperm and egg outside the body, to produce a pregnancy. It is called "in vitro" because this is Latin for "in glassware" – usually the fertilization happens in a glass-like dish or test tube.

The first IVF was performed on frogs, more than 250 years ago, when a scientist added frog sperm to frog eggs (frogspawn) in a pond. But frogs are usually fertilized in ponds, and they grow into babies there, too. Making IVF mammals is much trickier. These animals are usually grown inside the warmth of a body, which is a harder setting to recreate. The eggs are also a lot smaller than frogspawn – and can only be seen under a microscope.

Scientists first realised that mammals come from eggs in 1827, but mammal IVF was still believed to be impossible.

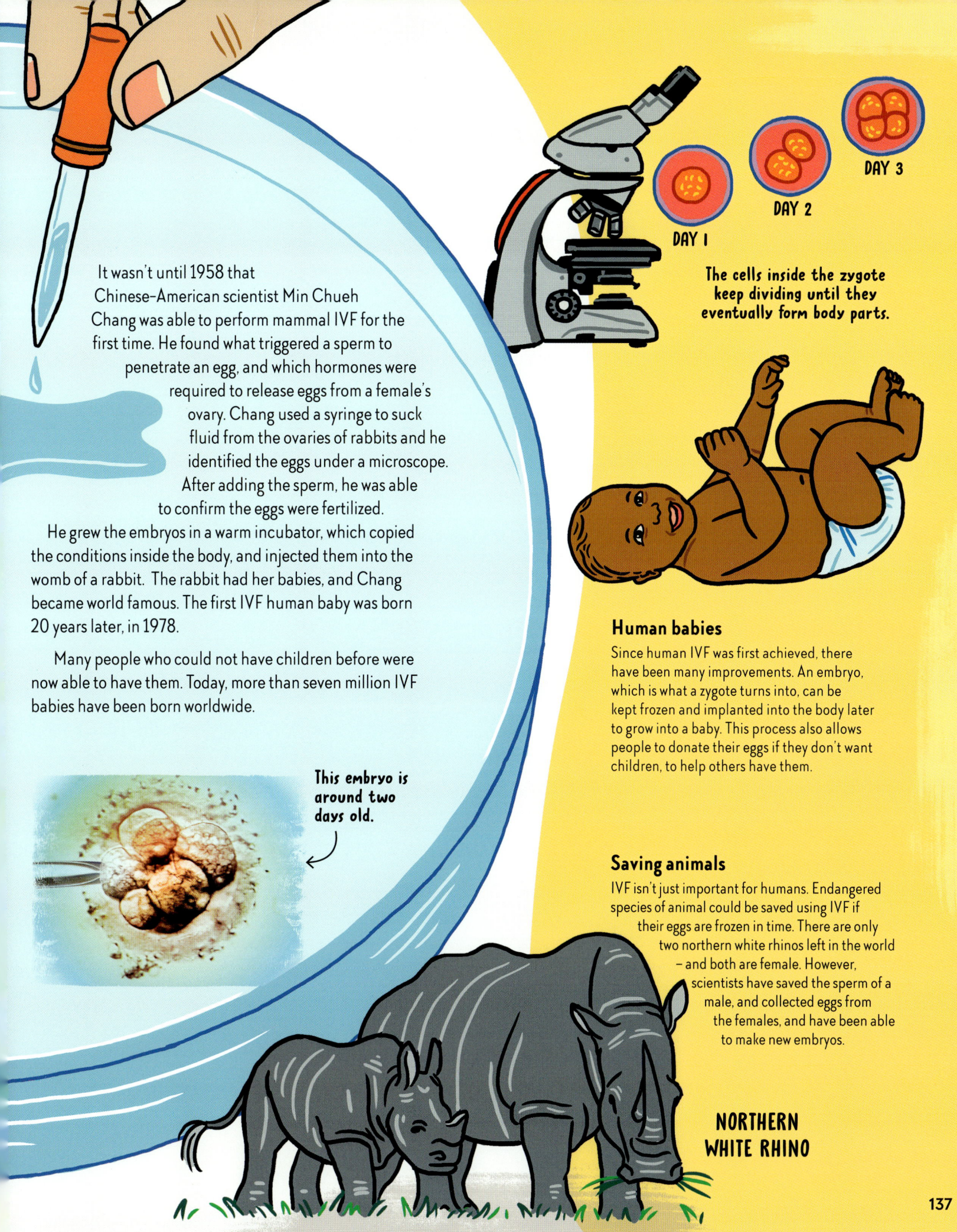

It wasn't until 1958 that Chinese-American scientist Min Chueh Chang was able to perform mammal IVF for the first time. He found what triggered a sperm to penetrate an egg, and which hormones were required to release eggs from a female's ovary. Chang used a syringe to suck fluid from the ovaries of rabbits and he identified the eggs under a microscope. After adding the sperm, he was able to confirm the eggs were fertilized.

He grew the embryos in a warm incubator, which copied the conditions inside the body, and injected them into the womb of a rabbit. The rabbit had her babies, and Chang became world famous. The first IVF human baby was born 20 years later, in 1978.

Many people who could not have children before were now able to have them. Today, more than seven million IVF babies have been born worldwide.

This embryo is around two days old.

DAY 1

DAY 2

DAY 3

The cells inside the zygote keep dividing until they eventually form body parts.

Human babies

Since human IVF was first achieved, there have been many improvements. An embryo, which is what a zygote turns into, can be kept frozen and implanted into the body later to grow into a baby. This process also allows people to donate their eggs if they don't want children, to help others have them.

Saving animals

IVF isn't just important for humans. Endangered species of animal could be saved using IVF if their eggs are frozen in time. There are only two northern white rhinos left in the world – and both are female. However, scientists have saved the sperm of a male, and collected eggs from the females, and have been able to make new embryos.

NORTHERN WHITE RHINO

CHAPTER 10

COMPUTERS

The abacus is the oldest computer and has existed for over 3,000 years. This simple wooden frame holds strings of beads in rows. It's cheap, portable, and there are no complicated bits of machinery that can go wrong.

Now, let's fast forward to the 1800s and Charles Babbage's invention of the Difference Engine. It cost millions in today's money, was quite slow, and you couldn't slip it in your pocket as it weighed seven tons. Yet this machine was revolutionary in its ability to solve complicated mathematical problems.

Via the internet, modern computers supply amounts of information that no human could retain. They tackle problems which would take many humans working together to solve. Progress in computing is moving extremely quickly, and computers that think like humans, called artificial intelligence, are the next step.

THE DIFFERENCE ENGINE

This machine paved the way for the computers we rely on today.

The Difference Engine, often regarded as the first ever mechanical computer, was a calculator designed to automate astronomical equations for use in navigation. It was designed in the 1820s and 30s by the gifted English mathematician Charles Babbage. Before its invention, all calculations were carried out manually, and often resulted in errors, which was very dangerous for sailors at sea.

By automating the construction of mathematical tables, Babbage was convinced of their accuracy. As it was such a complex and expensive design, the machine itself would not be completed. Babbage produced a prototype

as early as 1822, but kept adding elements and changing the design. Sadly, the Difference Engine was never completed in Babbage's lifetime, but it still paved the way for the modern computers, and Babbage is now known as "The Father of Computing".

Charles Babbage

Babbage later designed a second machine called an Analytical Engine, which would have been able to feed its own calculations back into itself, but it was also too expensive to be made.

What came next?

1945 ENIAC

During the Second World War, the Electronic Numerical Integrator and Computer (ENIAC) was designed to crack enemy codes. It was the first electronic computer, and many times faster than the existing mechanical devices.

1971 Microprocessors

A processor receives and decodes information in the computer, then instructs the device what to output in response. In the 1970s, the Intel 4004 microprocessor was released by Intel Corporation – it was roughly the size of a fingernail.

DIFFERENCE ENGINE

The language of computers

Computer programming is the process of writing instructions to be carried out by the computer, such as showing different words or images on the screen. These instructions are called 'computer code'. The English mathematician Ada Lovelace is credited with inventing the first computer code while assisting Charles Babbage with the design of his second machine, the Analytical Engine.

```
if (score >5) {
    showWinnerScreen()
    }
else {
    showGameOverScreen()
```

GAME OVER
play again?

1981 Personal computers

After the invention of microprocessors, computers could be built smaller and cheaper than ever before. This eventually made it possible for people to have them in their homes, and in 1981, IBM introduced the Personal Computer.

Nowadays, we are used to having personal laptops, which are portable and more lightweight.

ROBOTICS

The use of robotics is common in many areas of modern life. With improved engineering, better computerised design, and sophisticated programming, they change how we work and play. People are equally fascinated, delighted, and horrified by robots. How do you feel about them?

INDUSTRIAL ROBOTICS

Robotics revolutionised factory work. The Ford production line was the first example of an automated assembly line. Now, specially built robots carry out heavy, repetitive, and skilled work faster and more accurately than humans.

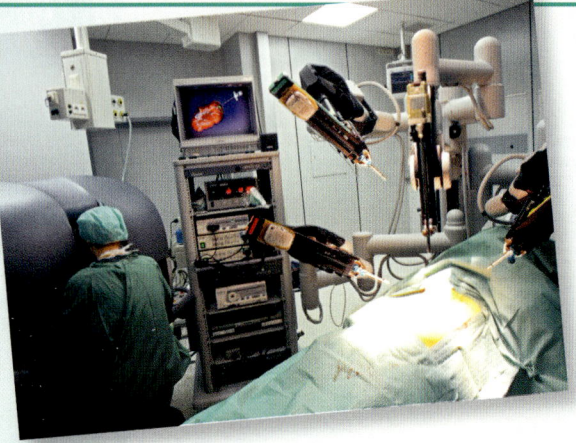

MEDICAL ROBOTICS

Most medical robots are controlled by surgeons. They carry out all sorts of procedures through tiny incisions, with a high degree of accuracy. The use of robotics in this way means that more operations can be done through "keyhole incisions", which usually have a much shorter recovery period.

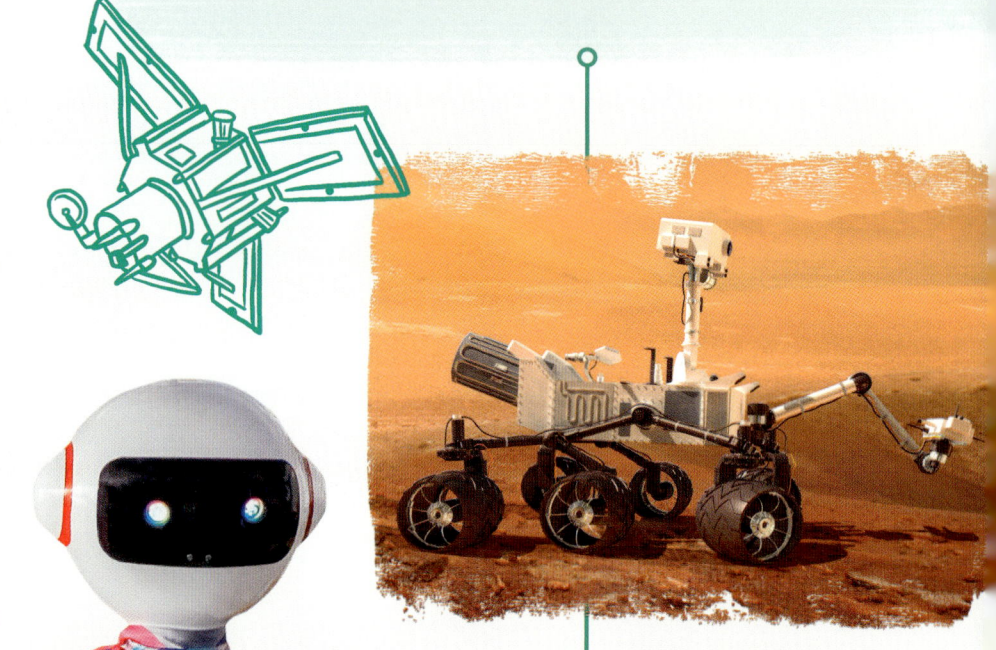

SPACE ROBOTICS

Sending humans to explore space is dangerous and expensive (spaceships are very heavy and so require huge amounts of energy to take off). Space robots avoid the risk to human life, are much cheaper, and can gather as much information as humans – if not more!

SERVICE ROBOTICS

Service robots are on the rise. Some will come in a humanoid shape and function as an assistant or waiter in real life; some will take on chores in the home, for example a robotic vacuum cleaner or lawn mower. Other service robots function as computer programmes, such as the automated chatbots you might find on a website.

AGRICULTURAL ROBOTICS

Farmers mostly use robots and machines for harvesting, and occasionally for weed control and preparing land. Drones are sometimes used to protect crops from pests and to monitor and respond to changes in the environment.

MILITARY ROBOTICS

Robotics are increasingly used by the military, for example for clearing minefields without risking human injury, or sending unmanned drones for reconnaissance missions. They can be used to carry and fire weapons, too.

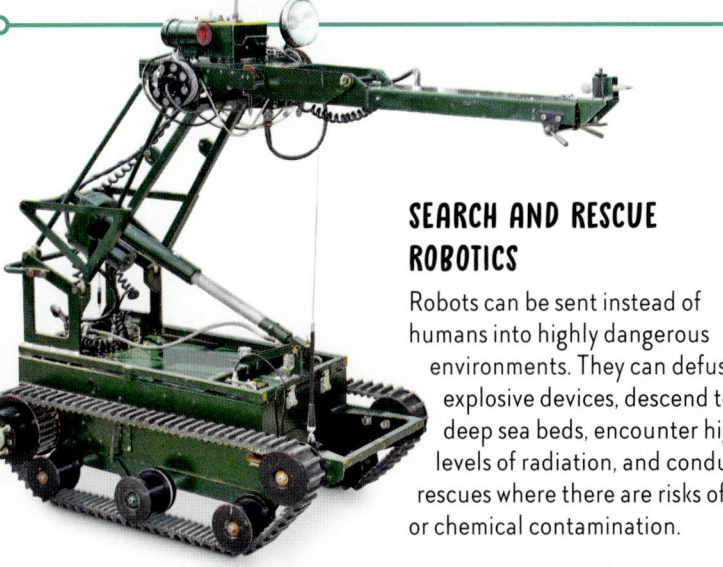

SEARCH AND RESCUE ROBOTICS

Robots can be sent instead of humans into highly dangerous environments. They can defuse explosive devices, descend to deep sea beds, encounter high levels of radiation, and conduct rescues where there are risks of fire or chemical contamination.

AUTONOMOUS VEHICLES

Did you know that the largest cause of vehicle accidents is human error? In some countries, driverless trains and cars are already operating, though many people feel uneasy about the thought of it. Would you fly in a pilotless plane? Statistically, it might be the safest option.

UNDERWATER ROBOTICS

Unmanned underwater vehicles are built to withstand the immense pressure of water in the deepest parts of the sea. They are often fitted with cameras and are sent to explore the seabed, often discovering new underwater species. Some deep-sea robots are used to gather data to help restore the ecosystems in specific underwater areas.

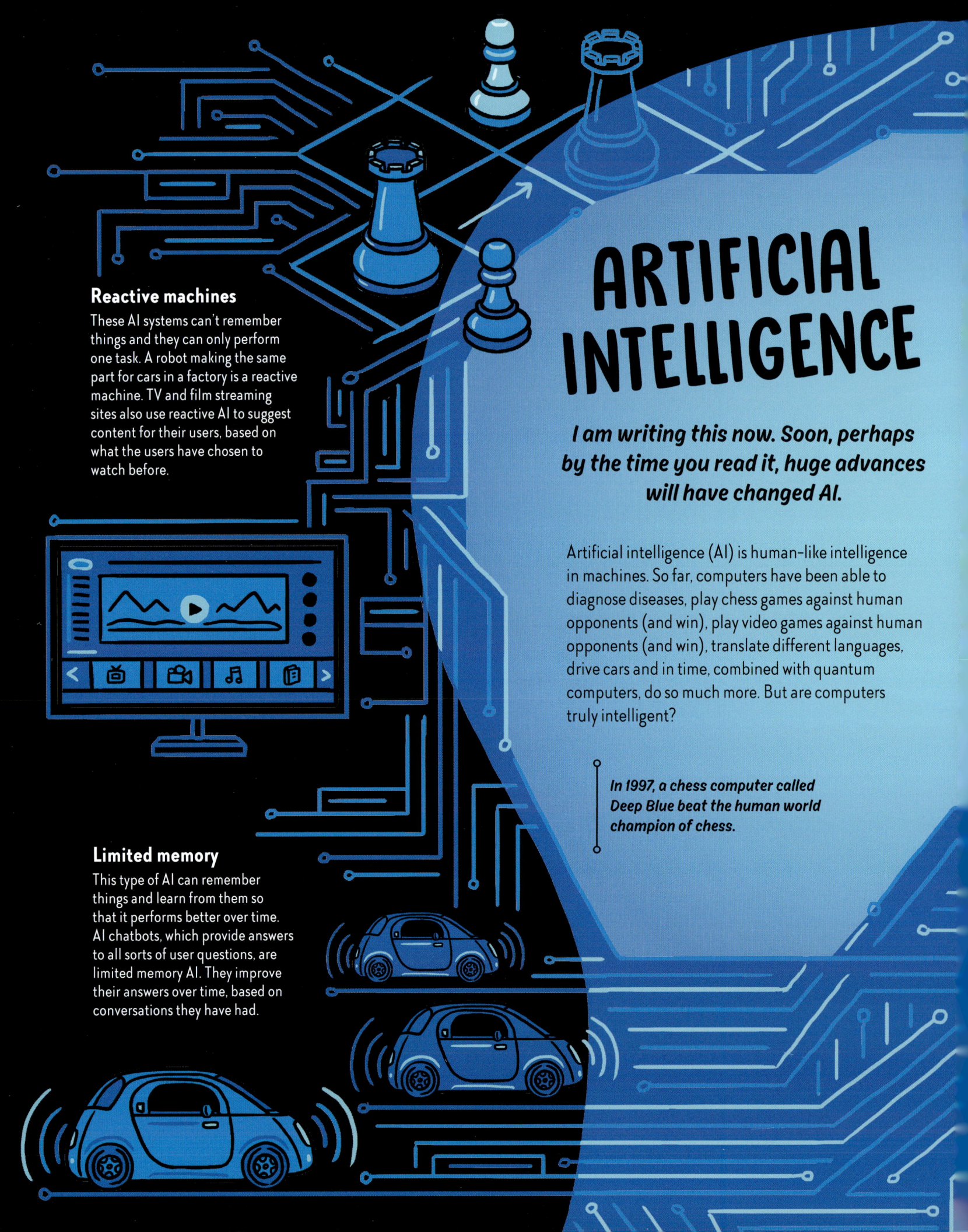

Reactive machines

These AI systems can't remember things and they can only perform one task. A robot making the same part for cars in a factory is a reactive machine. TV and film streaming sites also use reactive AI to suggest content for their users, based on what the users have chosen to watch before.

Limited memory

This type of AI can remember things and learn from them so that it performs better over time. AI chatbots, which provide answers to all sorts of user questions, are limited memory AI. They improve their answers over time, based on conversations they have had.

ARTIFICIAL INTELLIGENCE

I am writing this now. Soon, perhaps by the time you read it, huge advances will have changed AI.

Artificial intelligence (AI) is human-like intelligence in machines. So far, computers have been able to diagnose diseases, play chess games against human opponents (and win), play video games against human opponents (and win), translate different languages, drive cars and in time, combined with quantum computers, do so much more. But are computers truly intelligent?

In 1997, a chess computer called Deep Blue beat the human world champion of chess.

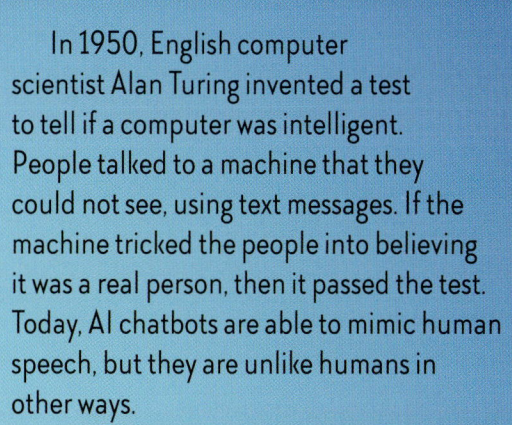

In 1950, English computer scientist Alan Turing invented a test to tell if a computer was intelligent. People talked to a machine that they could not see, using text messages. If the machine tricked the people into believing it was a real person, then it passed the test. Today, AI chatbots are able to mimic human speech, but they are unlike humans in other ways.

AI does not have the creative spark of humans – machines can only copy art that we have already done. Machines do not have emotions, either, which are an important part of human intelligence. And machines cannot make decisions based on emotions, like humans do .

But whatever AI lacks now, it is likely to improve upon in time. For the moment, we have a long way to go.

Theory of mind

This type of AI doesn't exist yet, but it will be able to interact with humans much better than previous AI because it will understand them better. Like humans, and unlike current AI, it will understand that the people around it have their own thoughts and emotions.

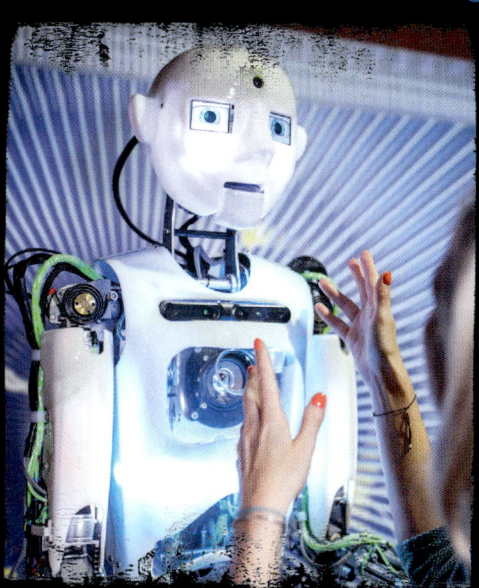

Self-awareness

The final step towards having human intelligence is for AI to develop its own feelings and goals, like you. Current AI chatbots may seem to have emotions, but this is because they have been trained using human speech and are simply copying the emotions that exist there. In fact, AI is definitely not self-aware. But many computer scientists think this will be possible.

MICROCHIPS

This tiny chip made today's computer technology possible.

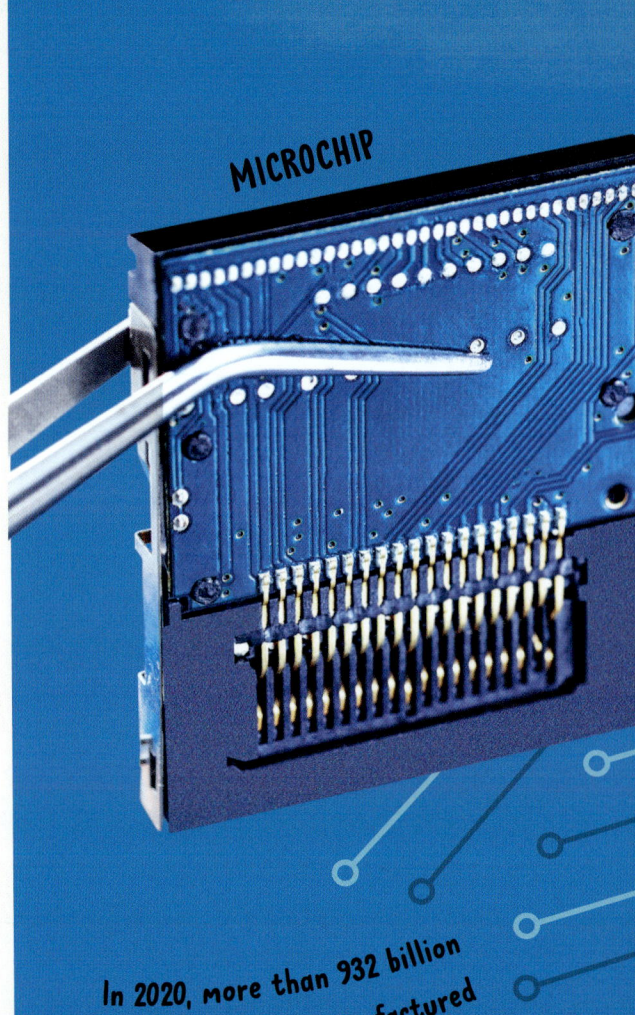

Computers were once big enough to fill entire rooms. The technology that instructed them to carry out tasks was too bulky to fit inside smaller machines. Then, in 1958, the US inventor Jack Kilby worked out a way to fit a huge amount of information onto a small, flat chip – the microchip.

Inside computers, electronic signals tell the machine what to do. The first computers used glass radio valves to create these electronic signals. Radio valves looked a bit like large lightbulbs and contained electrodes that passed electricity between them. Tens of thousands of valves were needed to build computers. The valves could grow very hot, they broke easily, and they used a lot of electricity. I tried to make my own radio valve when I was 11. I switched it on, it hummed alarmingly, there was blue smoke, and I burnt my fingers!

Luckily, in 1947, smaller devices called transistors were invented to create electronic signals. By the late 1950s, transistors were small enough to be used in tiny circuits on thin sheets of a semiconductor – a material that can both conduct and stop the flow of electricity, such as silicon. Sheets of the semiconductor could then be sandwiched together to form the small and mighty microchip.

Transistor

Today, the two main types of microchip are memory chips, which store memory, and logic chips, which contain instructions for the machine to carry out tasks. The first microchip was about the size of a pencil tip. Modern chips can be much smaller than a speck of dust.

In 2020, more than 932 billion microchips were manufactured around the world.

Pet chips are about the size of a grain of rice.

ACTUAL SIZE

What are microchips used for?

The microchips used today can be quite simple – some store a single number – or they can be complex enough to hold the memory of an entire computer. They are found everywhere, including in bank cards, mobile phones, smart cards, and even pets!

Pet chips store a number that can be matched to the owner if the pet is lost.

MICROCHIP
WITH CASING

The microchip casing
is usually made from
epoxy resin – a strong
form of plastic that
keeps the silicon
chip safe.

Metal pins
connect the
chip to the
other parts
of the machine.

What came next?

Microchips in space

The USA's NASA (National Aeronautics and Space Administration) used microchips to build the onboard computers of the Apollo spacecraft, which took astronauts to the Moon from 1969. The computers helped astronauts to navigate and to control the spacecraft.

Moore's Law

In 1965, microchips had only been around for about 15 years – but Gordon Moore. the co-founder of the computer brand Intel, knew how powerful they could be. He said that microchips would double their abilities every two years, whilst becoming ever smaller.

Human chips

A few people around the world have implanted chips beneath their skin. The chips store different types of information, such as digital money to pay for things. Chips inside humans are likely to become more popular, and future chips could link our brains to the internet.

Bank cards have chips
storing their owner's
bank details, to allow
the owner to pay for
things with a tap.

Chips in
smartphones
store memory
and control
the phone.

Modern cars contain
around 1,400 chips doing
lots of jobs.

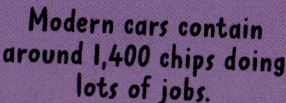

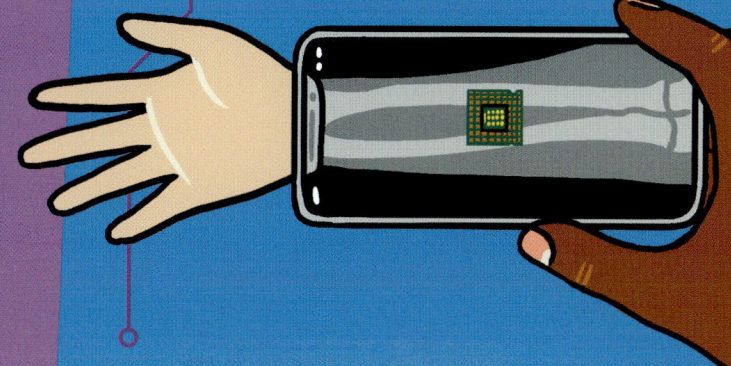

The Arpanet

The USA's ARPANET began as a network of four computers at different universities. The first cross-country connection was made in 1970 and the ARPANET became international in 1973, with a connection to the UK.

The ARPANET network in 1977

THE INTERNET

Connecting computers sparked a new age of information.

In 1963, a US psychologist and computer scientist called Joseph Licklider shared a grand idea – what if people around the world could be connected through their computers? Licklider called his dream network the Intergalactic Computer Network, but we now know it as the internet.

The earliest version of the internet was the ARPANET (Advanced Research Projects Agency Network), which was used from 1969. It connected computers at different universities in the USA using telephone lines. The network allowed researchers to share information about specialist subjects with each other. Each letter of text was split into small pieces of data, called bits, in order to be sent over the network.

Undersea cables

More than 99% of internet data is carried around the world through undersea cables. Huge amounts of data can travel from one continent to another in less than a second.

Inside the cable

Data centres

Websites are hosted on servers. When someone accesses the website from their device, the text, images, and videos are sent as bytes through cables or satellites from the server.

The World Wide Web

The web was invented in 1989. It is made up of the pages and websites that can be accessed on the internet. Websites have "WWW", for World Wide Web, at the start of their address.

Tim's computer

Tim Berners-Lee

Tim Berners-Lee, an English computer programmer, created the World Wide Web. He wanted user-friendly access to the internet with powerful ways to search for information.

The ARPANET grew to be international during the 1970s, but it still only included certain organizations, such as universities. Websites and the World Wide Web were invented in 1989, and the internet began to be used more widely in the early 1990s. Now, people could make their own internet pages about any topic they liked. The first photograph was put on the web in 1992, though it was very small – an image is made up of far more bits than text, and the internet was not powerful enough to send huge amounts of data. Eventually, new inventions, such as optical cables, increased the amount of data that could be sent.

Today, many people can access internet content from the palm of their hand, on smartphones. Sometimes, lies can be spread on the internet, but this special network has many good effects. It allows us to communicate instantly through emails, to learn through educational websites, to rent digital books from libraries, to watch films and sports, to play games, and to do much, much more.

Each letter sent over the ARPANET was made up of a packet of eight bits. The packet of eight became known as a byte, which is a unit often used for internet data today.

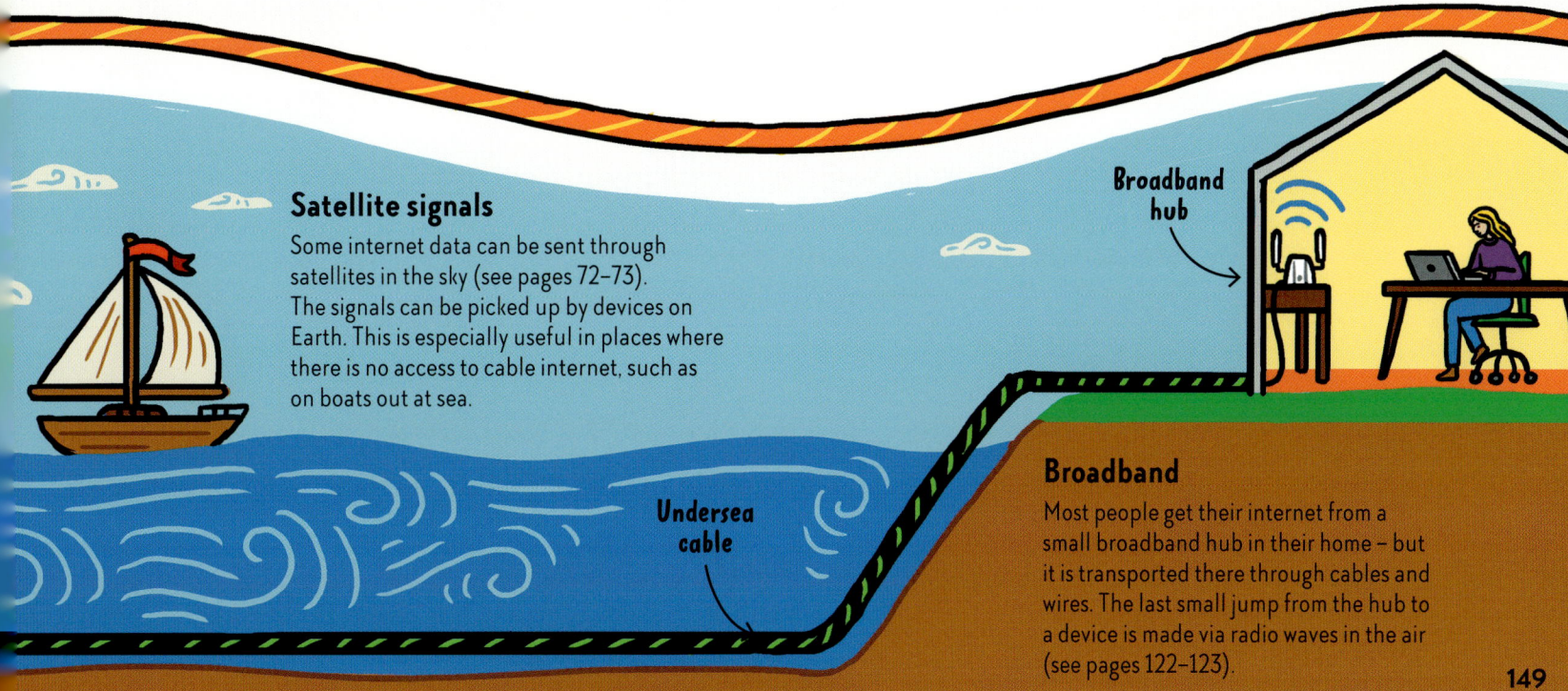

Satellite signals

Some internet data can be sent through satellites in the sky (see pages 72–73). The signals can be picked up by devices on Earth. This is especially useful in places where there is no access to cable internet, such as on boats out at sea.

Broadband hub

Undersea cable

Broadband

Most people get their internet from a small broadband hub in their home – but it is transported there through cables and wires. The last small jump from the hub to a device is made via radio waves in the air (see pages 122–123).

CONCLUSION

There is no doubt that scientific knowledge has improved our lives, immeasurably. But its use has also led to unpredictable harms. Climate change following the Industrial Revolution is just one example. Humans have also often misused science – the stories of weapons of war troubles everybody.

You definitely do not need to be a scientist (indeed, I do not want to persuade you to "do science") but good citizens should feel obliged to have some understanding of science, and this book is hopefully a small contribution to that.

The advances covered in this book happened because scientists wanted to improve things. But successful experiments never occur overnight – they all take a lot of effort. Experiments, observing what happened, and keeping careful records are crucial to science, and all require persistence.

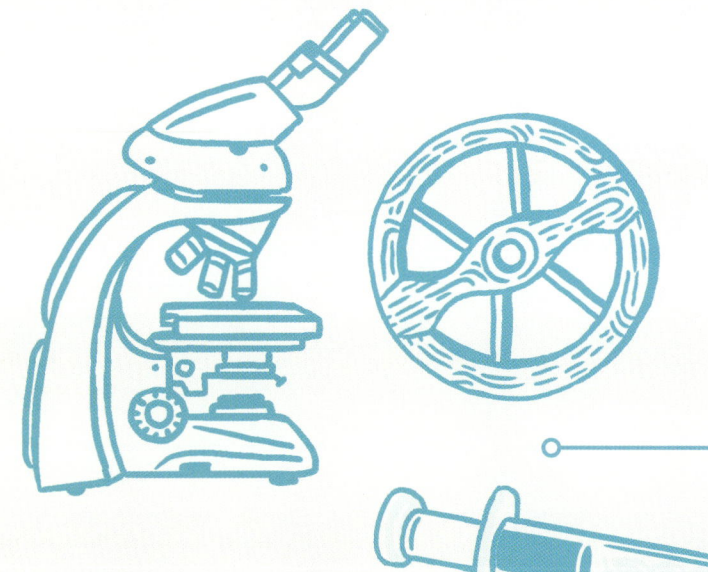

Don't worry about failure; it is most valuable – if we learn from it. All good scientists want to know why they failed and how to improve. Breakthroughs are seldom immediate, and constant practice gets better results. Most science is done together with other people. Not only is collaboration fun, but it is a huge advantage in most human activity, especially science. Sharing failure truthfully leads to success, and success leads to more success.

But science is only a part of understanding. We now explore artificial intelligence and risk making machines which could make independent decisions without the ethical values that human beings possess. This is one of the reasons that scientists should not ignore history or the arts – we all need to continue to read widely and remember that wide knowledge and wisdom makes you a better human, and better than a machine.

Value your humanity, think about what is ethical, and what might be unwise, and keep on searching, discussing, and learning.

– ROBERT WINSTON

GLOSSARY

ALCHEMY
Ancient form of study from which the study of chemistry developed

AMPUTATE
To cut off a body part for medical reasons, such as injury or infection

ARTIFICIAL
Made by humans and not found in nature

ASTRONOMY
The study of objects in space

ATOM
Tiny particle of matter. Atoms can bond together to form larger particles called molecules

BACTERIA
Microscopic single cells living in soil, water, or on the bodies of plants and animals

CELL
The building blocks of any living thing

CONDUCTOR
A material that allows electric current to flow through it. Metals are typically good conductors, while wood and plastic are not

CURRENT
A flow of electricity consisting of electrons moving through a material

DIAGNOSE
To work out the nature of an illness or problem through careful examination

DNA
Chemical that stores the information about how our bodies will grow and function

DOMINANT GENE
A gene that overpowers another gene

ECO-FRIENDLY
Something that does less harm to the environment than most alternatives

ELECTRICITY
A type of energy that can be used to power appliances such as lights. It is also found naturally as lightning

ELECTRODE
Part of a system for generating an electric current

ELEMENT
One of 118 known substances that make up all known materials, including minerals

ENERGY
A source of power such as electrical energy or heat energy

EVOLUTION
The development of a species over many generations as it adapts to its environment

FORCE
Something like push or pull that causes things to start moving, move faster, change direction, slow down, or stop

GENE
An inherited part of DNA that controls a specific function

GENOME
The complete set of information carried by all the genes in a living thing

LABORATORY
Place where various scientific experiments take place

LENS
A transparent material with a curved surface used to form images

MAGNETISM
Force created by magnets, which pull some metals towards them

MASS

The amount of matter that exists in an object

MATTER

Anything that has mass or takes up space – the stuff from which everything in the universe is made

MESOPOTAMIA

Ancient region in western Asia found in modern-day Iraq

MICROORGANISM

A living creature that is too small to see without the use of a microscope

MUTATION

A change to the DNA of a living thing, causing physical changes

NOMADIC

Living things that constantly move around rather than live in one place

NUCLEUS

The central part of an atom

PARTICLE

A tiny speck of matter, such as an atom or a molecule

PETRI DISH

A piece of lab equipment where scientists grow and cultivate microbes

POLLUTION

Substances that are harmful to the environment, such as by-products generated by factories, cars, and farming

RADIATION

Rays of energy emitted by certain elements, or materials they have interacted with

RECEIVER

Electronic device that receives signals

RECESSIVE GENE

A gene that is overpowered by a dominant gene

SATELLITE

An object (human-made or natural) that orbits around another object in space

SOLAR PANEL

A surface that creates electrical energy from the energy in sunlight

SOVIET UNION (USSR)

A Russian-led group of states that existed from 1922 to 1991. Also known as the USSR (Union of Soviet Socialist Republics)

SPECIES

Living things that have very similar genes, look alike and can breed with each other

SUBSTANCE

A particular type of material

THERAPY

Treatment designed to help with people's mental and physical health

TRANSMITTER

Electronic device that sends out signals

VACCINE

A type of medication that teaches the body's immune system to fight specific diseases

INDEX

ACKNOWLEDGEMENTS

DK would like to thank:

Ciara Finan from Curtis Brown. Helen Peters for Indexing. Sachin Gupta, Syed Tuba Javed, Vijay Kandwal, Roohi Rais, and Sakshi Saluja for picture library assistance.

Roberto Junior (bc). **92 Alamy Stock Photo:** TT News Agency / Bjorn Larsson Rosvall (b). **93 Dreamstime.com:** Johan Mollerberg (c). **94 Alamy Stock Photo:** Chronicle (tr); Pictorial Press (cl); GL Archive (bl); Everett Collection Historical (bc). **95 Alamy Stock Photo:** Associated Press / Anonymous (c); Pictorial Press (tl); Scherl / Sddeutsche Zeitung Photo (tc); GL Archive (br). **Getty Images:** AFP PHOTO / DPA / Christian Charisius / Germany Out (bl). **96 Alamy Stock Photo:** Anna Fotyma (cr). **97 Alamy Stock Photo:** Wirestock, Inc. (cl). **100 123RF.com:** Cristian Gusa. **102 Alamy Stock Photo:** agefotostock / Historical Views (cl, tc); Fine Art Images / Heritage Images (crb); Icom Images (bl). **103 Alamy Stock Photo:** Mauricio Abreu (cra); Granger, NYC (bl). **Getty Images / iStock:** fotorezekne (crb). **Science Photo Library:** Mathematical Association Of America (cla). **104 Alamy Stock Photo:** Penta Springs Limited / Artokoloro (ca). **106 Alamy Stock Photo:** Sibag (tr). **108 Dorling Kindersley:** Gary Ombler / HPS Museum of Leeds University (br). **Getty Images / iStock:** FlamingPumpkin (cra). **110 Dreamstime.com:** MartinBergsma (br). **Science Photo Library:** Royal Institution Of Great Britain (cra). **112 Dreamstime.com:** Antonella865 (cr). **116 123RF.com:** Marek Uliasz (cb). **118 Alamy Stock Photo:** Granger, NYC (bc). **Dreamstime.com:** Shijianying (cr). **119 Alamy Stock Photo:** World History Archive (clb). **120 Alamy Stock Photo:** World History Archive (tl). **121 Alamy Stock Photo:** Dotted Zebra (tl). **123 Alamy Stock Photo:** World History Archive (tl). **127 Alamy Stock Photo:** INTERFOTO / Personalities (tc). **128 Dreamstime.com:** Tom Wang (t). **130 Alamy Stock Photo:** agefotostock / Historical Views (b). **131 Alamy Stock Photo:** Tom Kidd (tl). **132 Alamy Stock Photo:** Pictorial Press (bc). **134 Alamy Stock Photo:** Charles Walker Collection (cl). **135 Alamy Stock Photo:** Antiqua Print Gallery (cr). **137 Alamy Stock Photo:** Science Photo Library / ZEPHYR (clb). **141 Dorling Kindersley:** Clive Streeter / The Science Museum (tl). **142 Getty Images:** Moment / Sumith Nunkham (tc). **Science Photo Library:** Henning Dalhoff (crb); Patrick Landmann (cl). **Shutterstock.com:** Stefano Mazzola (bc). **143 Dreamstime.com:** Baloncici (clb). **Getty Images:** Moment / Kypros (tr); Moment / Vithun Khamsong (cla); Photodisc / Mark Deeble and Victoria Stone (bl). **Science Photo Library:** Philippe Psaila (cr). **145 Alamy Stock Photo:** Westend61 (cr). **146 Dreamstime.com:** Sergey Chuyko (tr). **147 Depositphotos Inc:** Sashkin7 (tl). **148 Alamy Stock Photo:** Stefan Sauer / ZB / dpa (br). **160 Robert Winston** (c).

All other images © Dorling Kindersley.

Author Professor Robert Winston
Illustrator Caitlin Keegan
Consultant Stephen Haddelsey
Acquisitions Editor James Mitchem
Project Editor Kat Teece
Project Art Editor Charlotte Milner
Designers Hannah Moore, Bettina Myklebust Stovne, Sadie Thomas
Additional Editing Becca Arlington, Shari Black, Marie Greenwood, Abi Maxwell
Additional Design Ann Cannings
Managing Editor Jonathan Melmoth
Managing Art Editor Diane Peyton Jones
Production Editor Dragana Puvacic
Production Controller John Casey
Jacket and Sales Material Coordinator Magda Pszuk
Publishing Director Sarah Larter

First published in Great Britain in 2023 by
Dorling Kindersley Limited
DK, One Embassy Gardens, 8 Viaduct Gardens,
London, SW11 7BW

The authorised representative in the EEA is
Dorling Kindersley Verlag GmbH. Arnulfstr. 124,
80636 Munich, Germany

Text copyright © 2023 Professor Robert Winston
Artwork copyright © Caitlin Keegan 2023
Layout and design copyright © 2023
Dorling Kindersley Limited
A Penguin Random House Company
10 9 8 7 6 5 4 3 2 1
001–327016–Nov/2023

A CIP catalogue record for this book
is available from the British Library.
ISBN: 978-0-2415-3854-8

Printed and bound in Slovakia

www.dk.com

This book was made with Forest Stewardship Council™ certified paper – one small step in DK's commitment to a sustainable future. **For more information go to www.dk.com/our-green-pledge**

To my lovely grandchildren: Zeke, Grace, Stella, Tzofia, Eleanor, Aron, Ruby, and Isaac.

- ROBERT WINSTON

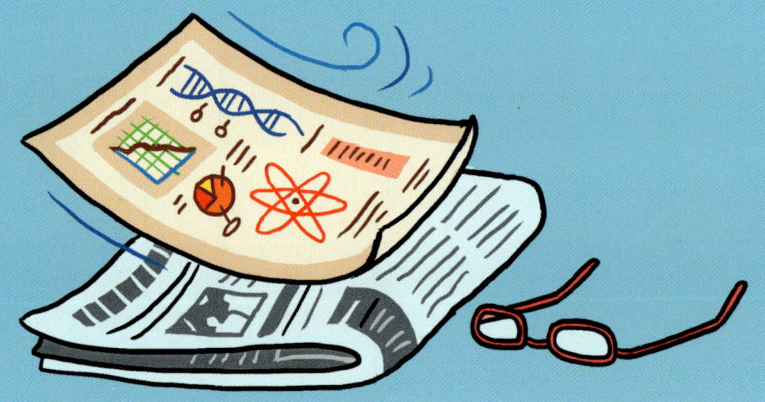